FERGIE:
THE VERY PRIVATE
LIFE OF THE
DUCHESS OF YORK

FERGIE:
THE VERY PRIVATE LIFE OF THE DUCHESS OF YORK

Madame Vasso
as told to David Leigh

Pinnacle Books
Kensington Publishing Corp.

http://www.pinnaclebooks.com

PINNACLE BOOKS are published by

Kensington Publishing Corp.
850 Third Avenue
New York, NY 10022

First Printing: December, 1996
10 9 8 7 6 5 4 3 2 1

Printed in the United States of America

To the memory of my mother,
a noble Grecian lady.

ACKNOWLEDGEMENTS

Many people have helped in the production of this book. I am grateful for the love, support and energy of my son, Nikos. Special thanks are due to my brothers, Kostas, Ioannis and Nicos for being there, always, when I needed them. The patience of David Leigh, without whom it would not have been possible, is greatly appreciated. My agent, Patrick Walsh, has been a wonderfully sensible adviser.

CONTENTS

CHAPTER ONE
HEALING HANDS

Glancing at the alarm clock beside my bed, I could see that it was almost three o'clock in the morning. The shrill ring of the telephone had woken me with a start but, as I sleepily reached over to pick up the receiver, I knew there was no need to ask who was calling. 'What is wrong, my baby?' I simply asked. 'Oh, Vasso, I'm sorry to wake you, but I just couldn't sleep,' the tearful voice at the other end of the line responded. 'I needed to talk to you so badly. I feel so lousy, so depressed. Sometimes I think the whole world is against me. Please tell me everything is going to be all right. I really don't know if I can take much more pain.' I told the girl to calm down and relax. 'I will fetch the cards to see what they can tell me,' I said. 'You must be strong. You must not let them beat you.'

We had met by chance several months earlier at the home of a mutual acquaintance. The friend, an elderly lady from my native Greece, had told her guest of the psychic powers I had possessed since I was a young child and how I had been gifted with 'healing hands' that enabled me to soothe away people's aches and pains.

I had taken my friend a gift of some Greek worry beads, brightly coloured blue stones threaded on a strip of leather that are really just decorative, although some people claim that rubbing them can help ease your worries. The girl said how lovely they were and, as I had another set in my bag, I pressed them into her hands and told her she must keep them. She seemed thrilled and, as I was leaving, she asked for my telephone number, saying, 'I would love you to tell me what the future holds for me. I must come and see you, I have so many things you may be able to help me with.'

She said she would ring but instead of using her real name, she would call herself 'Lady' — the name of one of her two pet Dalmatians, I discovered later — as she was worried about people listening in on her calls. The following day my telephone rang and, sure enough, it was 'Lady' saying she desperately wanted to see me. So we fixed an appointment for early the following Tuesday morning.

The doorbell rang shortly before 10 a.m. and there

on my doorstep stood Her Royal Highness the Duchess of York with one of her personal detectives. I had told her that she would have no difficulty finding my house — it was the only one in the street with large brightly coloured windmills and palm trees painted on the outside wall. This was common-place in my native Greece, but it stuck out like a sore thumb on a residential road in Islington, north London. Still, I liked the decoration as it constantly reminded me of home.

I was rather apprehensive at the thought of entertaining Royalty for the first time, and I wasn't quite sure what to expect, but I needn't have worried — Sarah was so down to earth that she made me feel totally at ease. She kicked off her shoes as she came though the front door and began admiring the many pictures adorning the hallway. 'I have lovely feelings about your house, it is so welcoming,' she told me. I thanked her and asked if she would like something to drink, but she responded, 'Vasso, you sit down. Tell me where everything is and I'll make us both a nice cup of coffee.' She wore a long, black polka-dot skirt and her flame-red hair was held back by a black velvet band. As she busied herself in the kitchen I thought how incredibly normal she seemed, not at all as I had expected. I was unsure about how I should address her, but she just laughed and said, 'Call me Sarah, that's what my friends call me. I can't be bothered with all that formal stuff with friends. That's for when I'm out performing!'

We chatted for a few minutes before I led her upstairs to my small healing room where I told her to sit down and relax. She told me she was born on 15 October, 1959, under the star sign of Libra, the sign of beauty and harmony. As with many Librans, I could see that she had a playful streak in her nature that she could never quite escape from and she laughed knowingly when I told her that Libran women were known for falling in love at the drop of a hat. It would not be long before I would discover that Sarah was certainly no exception.

As I began to read my special cards, which Sarah had shuffled and divided into four, I quickly realised that, emotionally, she was going through a very difficult stage in her life and there would be many more problems ahead. 'Spot on!' she exclaimed. Without any hesitation, she told me that her marriage was in desperate trouble, she felt totally neglected by her husband Prince Andrew and seriously doubted she could go on pretending that all was well for very much longer. I was taken aback, telling her that Andrew was a very handsome man who appeared to be kind and loving, but Sarah said, 'Vasso he's just not strong enough, he really isn't. He doesn't stand up for me when I need support and he's never there when I need him.'

However, I quickly discovered it wasn't Andrew that Sarah really wanted to talk about. 'Tell me what you can see about other men,' Sarah asked excitedly.

Clearing my mind and concentrating hard on the cards laid out on the small wooden table, I began to see another dark-haired man who would feature very strongly in Sarah's life. 'I can see another man, he is very handsome, dark and strong,' I said. Sarah admitted that there was someone else, someone special, an American called Steven. Again, I asked Sarah to shuffle the cards, but one of the first things I saw after choosing one for her American friend was a dark-haired woman beside him. In fact, there seemed to be more than one woman and I warned Sarah to be very careful as she risked being hurt. 'This man is a womaniser,' I warned. 'You must be careful because there are many women in his life.' Sarah responded, 'He's had lots of girlfriends, but I'm sure that's all in the past. He's so different from Andrew, so strong and considerate and he listens to what I have to say. I've never met anyone quite like him before. We're like soul mates who have so much in common — it's quite uncanny.'

We were virtual strangers, but over the next three hours Sarah poured out her many troubles while her personal detective waited patiently in my living-room downstairs. She wanted to know what the future held for her: would her children's books about Budgie the little helicopter be a success, and would she ever be able to leave Andrew? Above all, would she marry the

American and become Mrs Steven Wyatt?

Sarah added, 'Steven says he loves me, do you think it can be true?' I guessed that they were already far more than friends and asked if they were lovers. 'Yes,' she replied, 'we make love whenever we can. He's so wonderfully warm and passionate. Making love with Steven is like nothing on this earth.' Then she dropped the bombshell that they had first made love when she was five months pregnant with Andrew's second child. Sensing my shock, she added, 'I know it's awful, but Andrew just isn't interested in me any more. All he cares about is his work. Steven makes me feel so wanted. He is such a good lover. I miss him so much when we are apart.'

Sarah said it was the first time she had been unfaithful since taking her wedding vows, but she had no regrets. 'Steven says I am beautiful and wonderful and it makes me feel so good,' she told me. She was feeling neglected, unloved and alone and Steven was a shoulder to cry on; someone who was strong and made her feel attractive and loved again, but she was still hopelessly confused. 'My life is such a mess,' she said. 'Vasso, will it ever sort itself out?'

She told me about the hostility she had encountered from some members of the Royal Household and even some members of the Royal Family. 'Yes, it seemed like a fairytale once. How could it have gone so wrong?' she asked.

Eventually she had to leave, but said she would ring to make another appointment the following week. That evening, as I sat in front of my open fire, thinking over the day's events, the telephone rang. 'Hello, it's Lady,' said Sarah. 'I just wanted to thank you for being so patient and understanding today. It was a great help to me.' The following day she rang again and soon the phone calls became an almost daily occurrence as I learned the true depths of Sarah's despair.

But before taking a closer look at her life, I want to take you back to my childhood, to a small coastal village on mainland Greece, where, at an early age, it was discovered that I had strange psychic powers. It was there that I became known as 'the girl with blessed hands'.

CHAPTER TWO
EARLY YEARS

I was born Vasiliki Kortesis on 6 June, 1938, in the tiny village of Kambos, on the outskirts of the town of Nafpaktos, on mainland Greece. This was an area with strong Egyptian influences that dated back to the 1820s. I was named after my grandmother, but everyone called me 'Vasso' for short. Settlers called the area the 'Spring of Magic' and many who live there today still believe it has mystical and magical qualities.

At least three or four times every year I return to the home I have kept in the village to visit my family and loved ones and soak up the peace and tranquillity of the area that gives me so much strength for my healing work.

During my early childhood years, I saw little of my father. He was a prison governor who worked long and hard and was frequently away from home for weeks at a time. So it was left to my mother, Katerina, and my two beloved grandmothers to raise the children. I was the oldest, born an hour before my twin brother Kostas, then there was Ioannis, my sister Vangelia and Nicos, the baby.

My mother was a very proud woman who worked hard to supplement my father's income. From a very young age I learned of the enormous power of the Egyptian pyramids and how their strength could be used to help others. When we played, we would often use sticks to build little wooden pyramids.

I was just two years old when my family realised that I was different from the other children of the village. It was during World War II and I was returning from a shopping trip to Nafpaktos with my mother and her sister. As we approached a bridge leading to the village, I amazed them by shouting, 'Run, run, run!' — my first ever words. My mother wondered what on earth was going on, but she scooped me into her arms and we ran across the bridge. When we reached the other side, my mother and aunt laughed at the fuss and continued the journey home.

However, later that day, their blood ran cold when they learned that less than an hour after we crossed it, the bridge had been razed to the ground by a wave of bombs from German war planes.

..................*

My mother was an incredibly kind woman, respected by villagers for her healing powers. Whenever one of our family, friends or neighbours was ill, she would cure them with special medicines and creams she made from herbs that grew around the village.

Both my grandmothers were a major influence on my childhood years. I was a free spirit who, rather than play with other children, would spend many hours watching my grandmothers massage the necks and backs of friends and neighbours who came to them suffering from aches and pains. This was an art that had been passed down through their families for generations. My maternal grandmother patiently taught me the secrets and techniques of massage, and how to use oils soaked in various garden herbs to treat different kinds of problems, such as arthritis or chest pains. When it was my turn to practise what I had learned, she would tell me she could feel the heat from my hands as I gently rubbed her neck.

Word of my healing abilities spread, and the many people who came to me always left saying that my touch had worked wonders. The people of Kambos soon proclaimed that the young Kortesis girl had 'blessed hands'.

* .... * .... *

I loved my village with its beautiful views out to sea. I would run around bare-footed without a care in the world, asking and wanting for nothing, helping my mother and grandmother and enjoying life to the full.

Our house had just two rooms — my parents' bedroom and the large open living-room that doubled as a bedroom for the rest of the family. An open fireplace provided the only heat.

Every April, as was the local custom, I would help my mother paint the walls of the house and the steps leading from the street with a fresh coat of white paint in preparation for the Greek Easter. Like all the other villagers, we were a close-knit family who stood by each other, no matter what.

I adored my brothers and sister and they always looked to me, as the eldest, to sort out their troubles. And so, when I was eight years old, I was devastated when my father decided it would be in my best interests to go to stay in Athens with wealthy friends. He believed that I would have a better upbringing and a proper education there.

To a child of such tender years, it seemed like a terribly harsh decision, but it was my father's wish and so I went, leaving behind my friends and family. I remember the feeling of fear and bewilderment when I said goodbye to my mother as she left me alone aboard the ferry at Nafpaktos that would be met in Athens by my father. I think I must have cried for most of the way there because, when I arrived, my eyes were red and swollen.

Waiting at the ferry terminal with my father was my 'uncle' Nikos Vlamis — who, I was told, had an important job in the city — and his wife, Tina, a beautiful Romanian princess who was said to be blessed with psychic powers. Tina had a daughter from a previous marriage, but she had married and left home, so Nikos and Tina divided their time between their two large houses in Athens — one in the heart of the city for the winter months, and the other on the outskirts, where they would spend the summer.

My father told me that they would look after me as if I was their own daughter, send me to a good school and make sure I would want for nothing. At the time, he was working in Athens but, because he was living alone in a small, rented room and working very long hours, there was no way I could stay with him. Besides, in a few months' time he would be leaving the city, as his work as a prison governor meant he had to move to a different jail every six months to ensure that no familiarity built up with the prisoners, many of whom had been jailed for their political beliefs.

Nikos and Tina may have told my father that they would treat me as a daughter, but it soon became obvious to me that what they really wanted was someone to run around after them, to clean the house and to fetch the shopping. They made me wear black shoes and a black dress with a white collar and apron, so I even looked like a servant.

I had my own little room on the ground floor, next to the kitchen, and there — alone and desperately unhappy — I would cry myself to sleep every night.

Every morning, I got up at the crack of dawn to begin my daily routine of chores, cleaning the house from top to bottom, washing the floors until they were spotless, a never-ending circle of dusting and polishing. Tina was a very hard woman who worked me to the bone. If she was not satisfied with the job I had done, I had to do it again and again until she was happy. I was tiny then, and sometimes I was unable to reach things, which for some reason infuriated her. Heaven help me if I made a mistake, for I knew I would be punished with a slap, or sometimes worse.

My father would visit me whenever he could — usually on Sundays — but, apart from that, I had no contact with my family. I told him how unhappy I was, but he would always get very cross and tell me how ungrateful I was so, in the end, I decided it was better to keep my grief to myself.

Many months passed before he brought my mother to see me and she was obviously very shocked at what she saw. Her once happy and carefree daughter seemed so miserable. She told my father it was as if the life had been drained from my body. She saw my tiny hands, red and raw from the hours spent scrubbing and cleaning, and begged him to allow me to come home. He was angered that his judgement was being questioned and told her to give it a little more time and everything would work out for the best. My mother and I were in tears as we hugged each other goodbye. I could see so much hurt in her eyes, but she dared not let my father down, no matter how much it distressed her.

My guardians' winter home had a large balcony, surrounded by the beautiful pink and white roses that climbed the white-washed walls of the house. If I stood on the balcony, I could just about see the large screen of the outdoor cinema across the road and the little old lady, always dressed in black, who watched the door and slept in a ramshackle shed beside the building. No matter what time of the day it was she always seemed to be there.

One day, on my way back from the shop with the bread and yoghurt I had been sent to collect, I stopped to say hello to her. She said she had often seen me standing on the balcony and was pleased to meet me at last. She seemed so kind, yet I could tell from her old, frayed clothes that she was very poor. We became good friends and I would sit and talk with her — whenever I could sneak out of the house — and bring her sweets that I took from my uncle's drawers. I would tell her my problems and she would always tell me to be strong and manage to lift my flagging spirits. I often thought that she was my only friend in the world.

My birthday always passed unnoticed, although there was a small celebration on my saint's day — probably because it was also New Year's Day. Instead of receiving the proper education my parents had been promised, my only schooling came from my 'uncle' who patiently taught me to read and write. Nikos' father was a wealthy doctor, a good-natured, friendly man. I would often hear stories of how, when he visited poor patients, he would slip enough money under their pillow to enable them to buy the medicines he prescribed. I was never sent to school because that would have interrupted my work in the house and Tina considered herself too much of a lady to do it herself. She ruled the roost, and Nikos would do everything in his power to ensure that she got what she wanted.

Two or three times a week, some of Tina's wealthy friends would visit to play bridge and, before they went, she would usually do a tarot reading for them. I was fascinated by these cards. When I was about ten years old, Tina began to teach me about them, telling me to concentrate very hard and to say whatever came into my thoughts. She was impressed with what I saw, and believed I had a natural gift. Soon, she began to get me to do readings for her friends. Sometimes we would use different types of cards, each one emblazoned with a different face — some male, some female, some dark and some fair. I would choose a card that appeared most like the woman for whom I was doing the reading and then concentrate on it. The women always wanted to know if I could see any men in their lives and, if so, were they rich and successful. Sometimes I would see a man's face and then I would choose another card to represent him.

Tina also taught me more than 40 prayers and said it was important that I pray every morning and night, which I always did and still do to this day. But if she was such a religious lady, I used to think, why did she have to chastise me when I made a mistake?

..................*

I was about twelve years old when I decided to run away. It was summer and we were living on the outskirts of the city, but I managed to make my way to the centre and found the old lady who looked after the cinema. She was very worried and would let me spend only one night with her, because she told me that there would be terrible trouble if my uncle discovered what she had done. Nikos alerted my father to my disappearance and, after hours of frantic searching, they arrived at the cinema the following day. My father was furious that I had run away and caused such a commotion. He demanded that I apologise to Nikos and Tina and promise not to do anything so stupid again. I knew there was little point in protesting. My father failed to understand how I could be so ungrateful to people who had taken me in and given me a home, so I did as he said.

However, three years later, when I was fifteen years old, I decided that I could no longer put up with the unhappiness and ran away again, although this time it would be for good. I made my way to a convent on the outskirts of Athens, where the nuns agreed to give me temporary shelter after I told them about the years of misery. After four days they contacted my father who, sick with worry, rushed to the convent to collect me and finally take me home to Kambos.

I spent five wonderful weeks there with my family. My mother wept, blaming herself for everything that had happened to me and for allowing her own daughter to become a servant. I was not angry with her and told her she should not blame herself. I was just happy to have my life back again, to be free.

It was decided that I should return to Athens, as there was no work in the village and the prospects were not good. However, this time I would live with my father and my twin brother Kostas, who would work while he continued his studies in mechanical engineering. We rented a very small house and I quickly managed to find work as a machinist in a knitting factory. Early every morning, my father would drop me at the factory and pick me up on his way home from work. I worked long hours and, in the evening, I would do embroidery and cook and wash for my father and brother, but at least I knew that there would be no trouble if I did something wrong.

After a year, it was decided that my mother and the rest of the family should move to Athens. So we found a larger house and once again became a family. I was very happy, because although I worked hard, I had around me the people I loved.

It was around this time that I began courting. Michalis was ten years older than me and when my father found out, he was furious. He discovered, through his job with the prisons, that the man seeing his daughter had once been arrested during a political demonstration and he demanded an end to the relationship. 'I forbid you from seeing this man, he is nothing but a troublemaker,' my father told me. 'How do you think it would look for me if people found out that my daughter was involved with a man like this?'

I made promises to my father but had no intention of breaking off the relationship and so, from then on, our meetings had to be kept secret. The highlight of my week would be when Michalis took me to the theatre, which we both loved. We remained good friends for well over a year, but gradually we saw less and less of each other until we finally drifted apart.

I was 24 years old when I had a psychic experience that saved my brother's life. Ioannis was just 19 when he signed up with a merchant shipping company at the port of Piraeus, near Athens, and was due to join the crew of the cargo vessel, the *Aigli*. It was carnival time in Greece, with everyone in high spirits and enjoying themselves, but when Ioannis told me of his plans I was immediately struck with fear.

'Please do not go, I sense terrible danger ahead,' I told him. Ioannis had given the ship his papers and had been told to be ready to sail in two days. It was then that I told him not to go to sea on the *Aigli*, saying 'If you board that ship, you will die.' I had always had an almost telepathic understanding with Ioannis; he respected my psychic powers and so he assured me that he would heed my warning.

On 16 February, 1963, Ioannis joined another ship, the *Armonia*, which was owned by the same company and bound for Scotland and then on to the USA. Two days into his journey, he received news that the *Aigli* had sunk as it headed for home loaded with ore from Salonika. Just one member of the crew was saved, the remaining 21 lost their lives. Ioannis lost a lot of young friends and he later told me that when he heard the news, he felt empty. 'I should have been on the boat with them, but it was your warning that stopped me,' he said.

Ioannis, who now lives in a small flat in the port of Nafpaktos with his English-born wife, Laura, and their three children — the youngest of whom, Maria-Jane, aged 11, is believed to possess some of my mystical powers — tells friends: 'I never doubted Vasso's powers after that day. Today when I talk about the *Aigli*, I feel as empty as I did 30 years ago. Vasso possesses a gift that no one can explain. But her gift to me was my life. For that I will always be grateful.'

On 6 June, 1963 (my 25th birthday), I boarded a plane to London for what should have been a brief stay with Ioannis, who was living in a small, rented flat in Camden Town. Instead, it turned out to be a major turning point in my life, for I quickly decided to make London my home.

My brother had invited me to stay after I unwittingly became involved in a political demonstration in Athens. I was on my way to the theatre when I found myself in the midst of angry demonstrators trying to win free education for all Greek students. One young man had been knocked to the ground and, as I went to help him, the police arrested me as a witness and gave me a terrible hiding. I was named in the newspapers as a political activist, a troublemaker, and Ioannis, alerted by my family, invited me to stay with him for a few weeks until the trouble had blown over.

My first few years in London were incredibly hard. When I arrived, I had very little English and no formal qualifications. I was forced to take two or three menial jobs, knitting or embroidering, to make a decent living. I married — a brief and unhappy affair — and gave birth to my son Nikos, whom I cherish and adore. Struggling to bring up my son, I earned a little extra cash by doing readings for people who came to me for help or advice. Word quickly spread and soon most of my spare time was taken up with doing readings for friends and neighbours, who came to me after hearing about my psychic powers. Every day, a steady stream of people would turn up on my doorstep asking for help and advice or wanting a reading, usually to know if they were going to be lucky in love. Eventually, I set up a little market stall because I was worried about the number of people coming to my home, many of whom I didn't know. In 1988, I moved to the house in Islington that is still my home today.

..................*

Pyramids had always been a strong influence on my life, but it was not until I moved to my new home that I decided to have my own personal pyramid built in my small healing room, which is only seven foot square. The blue, perspex pyramid — blue is my personal healing colour — sits on a wooden frame, and is just tall enough to allow me to sit underneath it on a low wooden stool. Neither nails nor metal are used in the construction, as these would counteract the positive energy.

When I sit underneath the pyramid, I feel a surge of

energy transfer through my hands to whoever I am healing. For instance, if the person has back, neck or knee pains, I place my hands either directly on or over the painful area. Usually, within a few seconds, the person will feel the heat from my hands fill them with energy. What actually happens is that I extract the negative energy with my left hand and supply positive energy with my right. Sitting under the pyramid greatly increases the energy I am able to transfer. My hands are the most important element in my healing, as it is through them that all the energy flows. It is also very important for me to feel positive within myself, so I always spend a few minutes in private prayer before starting the healing.

People will often say to me, 'Your hands are burning', but I have no control over this warmth nor do I create it — it's just there. Some people expect miracle cures but I am not a miracle worker nor would I ever claim to be. I have helped numerous people over the years, but that is through having faith in God and faith in what I do. People must have faith to enable themselves to be helped; without it, they are wasting their time.

Among those who have visited me are business people with problems ranging from wanting to ensure their company's success and long-term future, to seeking ways of creating a better working environment for unhappy or unsettled employees. Sometimes I have felt the need to visit a particular workplace to get a feel of the surroundings and pick up any bad signals. One wealthy American woman, who was experiencing business difficulties, insisted on flying me out to visit her factory in the USA. She told me later that my suggestions for creating a healthier working environment had led to a turnaround in the company's success and that she would be always grateful for my help.

People who have turned to me for help and advice include powerful politicians, sportsmen and women, showbiz celebrities and their families, and, of course, Royalty.

The Duchess of York recommended me to friends and acquaintances including Linda Campbell, wife of the BBC Radio One disc jockey and TV game-show presenter Nicky Campbell. Sarah had read a newspaper article in which Linda spoke of her fight against the debilitating illness ME, which often confined her to bed for days at a time. Sarah found her telephone number and suggested that she visit me. 'She's a wonderful faith healer — why don't you give it a try?' Sarah asked her. Linda came to see me and later gave another interview in which she said: 'Vasso worked a miracle on me. Since my treatment I've got stronger and stronger and now I feel absolutely great.' Of course, I had not worked a miracle but, through my healing hands, the energy from the pyramid gave her the will to tackle the illness and convinced her to have faith.

My only aim in life is to help people by making them help themselves. If I can do that, then I am happy for I know what I have done has been worthwhile. Over the years, many doubters have left my home far less cynical than when they arrived.

CHAPTER THREE
LOVE AND MARRIAGE

On Sarah's second visit to my home, she brought along a photo of Steven in a small silver frame, believing it would help when I was doing a reading. Studying the picture, I admitted that he was indeed a handsome man, to which Sarah replied, 'I know, I know, but you wait until you see him in the flesh. He's a hundred times better.' She told me that she always kept the photograph with her as it was her way of keeping in close spiritual contact with Steven: 'As long as I've got this, I feel that he's never far away.'

Standing the photograph on the table, I dealt out the cards as Sarah sat opposite, anxiously waiting for what I could see. Again, I saw the images of at least two different women beside her new lover and I warned Sarah to be careful. 'These other women will not go away,' I told her. 'I know it is not what you want to hear, but I fear that Steven has other women in his life.' The concern showed in Sarah's face, but she tried to reassure herself that it couldn't possibly be true by telling me, 'There were other women but they've gone, I'm sure they have. He says I'm the only one in his life, Vasso, and I believe him. I'm sure if you met him you'd feel differently.'

Over the following months, Sarah would come to see me whenever she could. There were never any airs or graces. After exchanging kisses at the front door and taking off her shoes, she would breeze into my living-room and plonk herself down in one of the large comfortable chairs or lie on the sheepskin rug in front of the open fire. 'What a week!' she would say. 'You'll never believe what's happened since I last saw you.' And usually she was right: the woman known to millions across the world as 'fun-loving Fergie' never ceased to amaze me.

No sooner had she sat down than she would be on her feet again and into the kitchen, lifting the lids off the pans bubbling away on the cooker. Sarah loved her food, so I would always prepare some special Greek cakes whenever I knew she was coming. After a coffee and a chat to catch up on the latest news, we'd go upstairs to my healing room where Sarah's mood would quickly change.

She always entered the house bright and cheerful, as

if she hadn't a care in the world. But as soon as we sat down together inside the healing room, she would immediately start to tell me of her troubles, blurting out all that had gone wrong since we last met or spoke on the telephone. There was never a shortage of things to talk about.

During those early visits to my home, Sarah often asked if she would ever leave Andrew and marry Steven. I would tell her to put such notions out of her head because, in the long run, she would be far better off with her husband. 'You are having an affair, these things happen,' I told her, 'but at the end of the day, it is only an affair. You must remember that you are still a married woman and you have responsibilities. Affairs have a habit of fizzling out, but marriage is a much stronger bond. At the moment you are going through a bad time, but you both have a lot of growing up to do. In the end, this affair may make you realise how important your marriage is, especially for the sake of your children. Please, please be patient and don't do anything you will later regret.'

Sarah would often reminisce about her childhood and tell me how her mother had fallen in love with the Argentinian polo player Hector Barrantes. It was all the more hurtful for her father, Major Ronald Ferguson, as he had often fought bitter battles with Barrantes on the polo field. Both were top-class players and when their games ended, they always shared a laugh and a drink.

Sarah's father had considered the Argentinian to be a good friend.

Sarah was just fourteen years old when her beloved parents went their separate ways, and it had a profound effect on the lives of both her and her elder sister, Jane. As is common with many children of divorced parents, Sarah grew up feeling fractured and insecure, wondering whether she was in some way to blame for her parents' parting. Sarah, who stayed with her father, told me that it was the same for Princess Diana who also had to undergo the transformation from a girl to a woman without her mother's help.

Sarah was very close to her father, whom she called 'dads', turning to him whenever she was in trouble and seeking his advice whenever a problem arose. He was the dominant figure during her difficult teenage years and I believe this is why she has sometimes turned to a father-like figure when seeking the love and affection she constantly craves.

Her first true love, Paddy McNally, a former racing driver, was a widower and 22 years her senior when they began romancing in the early 1980s at the Swiss resort of Verbier. 'Paddy was great, he taught me so much about life,' Sarah told me. 'Whenever I wanted advice, I turned to him because he was so worldly wise. He seemed to have seen and done everything.'

They had a long and happy affair, punctuated by all the usual rows that blight relationships, but Sarah eventually left Paddy for Andrew when he told her he couldn't give her the long-term commitment she so desperately wanted. But they remained on good terms, and Sarah even invited him to her wedding, raising a few eyebrows in Andrew's camp and leaving the Prince's pride just a little bruised. Today, they remain good friends and Sarah knows Paddy is always just a phone call away if she needs someone to talk to. 'He's a true friend,' Sarah told me. 'He lets me and the girls use his chalet in Verbier whenever I want to go skiing. It saves me a fortune!'

In her heart, Sarah has always felt bitter that her mother chose to begin a new life in South America. Although they get on well now, Sarah still cannot understand how a mother could leave two teenage children and, for that reason, she has never totally forgiven her. 'I could never leave my girls, Vasso, they're far too precious to me. I really don't know how she could have gone off like that. I can't imagine being so far away from my babies and not being able to see them for months on end.' It was for this reason that Sarah was all the more concerned about her affair with Steven, terrified she might lose custody of the girls.

Sarah also told me how well she got on with the Queen throughout her engagement and marriage to Andrew. She laughed as she recalled a conversation they had had about her and Andrew's apartment at Buckingham Palace. 'The Queen asked how I liked it and I said it was wonderful, especially as I now had my own wardrobe! She seemed a bit surprised and I had to explain that in my previous flat, I had to hang my clothes on a rail similar to those used for shop displays. She thought it was hilarious.' Sarah told me that the Queen had a marvellous sense of humour and loved it when she repeated the latest jokes. 'Andrew's so like his mother when he laughs,' she told me. 'They both seem to like me telling jokes.'

I quickly discovered that Sarah suffered a great deal from stress, which was often pent up in knots in her neck and back. I would gently massage her to ease the strains away. She told me that she could feel the heat from my hands as I held them at either side of her head, filling her with energy. 'I don't know what you do, but it always makes me feel so much better, so much stronger,' she would tell me. Often, she was so relaxed that she almost drifted off into a deep sleep. I explained that that was due to the power of my healing. 'When I am with you, I feel as if I am in another time, in another place where I have no worries and no one gets me down,' she told me. 'It is as if my problems just disappear. It's just a shame I can't feel like that all the time!'

Sarah would phone me and sometimes we would speak for more than an hour, sometimes for ten minutes and sometimes she would just plead with me to stay by the telephone later that evening as she desperately needed a reading. She would think nothing of waking me in the early hours because she couldn't sleep and needed to know there and then what the cards could tell her. 'Oh, Vasso, please tell me what's going to happen, what's to become of me and Steven?' she would ask. She was desperate for good news, for me to tell her that everything would be fine, but frequently what I saw in the cards troubled me a great deal. I begged her to be careful as she had already suffered so much hurt and distress. Sarah knew I was right, but when I told her things she didn't like, she simply blotted them out of her mind. She knew she was taking a terrible chance conducting an affair when her every move was constantly scrutinised by the world's Press. Tongues were already beginning to wag and inside Buckingham Palace there was alarm and disapproval from those who sensed that Sarah and Steven's relationship may not be as innocent as she would have them believe.

CHAPTER FOUR
SUNNINGHILL AND THE PALACE

When Sarah was unable to visit me, she would sometimes invite me to her home, Sunninghill Park House, or her private apartments at Buckingham Palace. At the Palace, a police officer would confirm my name at the main gate and direct me to a side entrance where I would be met by a footman. I was then led to the most luxurious lift I had ever encountered (there was even an arm chair) and on through what seemed like a never-ending maze of passages that led to Sarah and Andrew's rooms in the East Wing on the second floor, overlooking The Mall. The red-carpeted hallways were furnished with huge wooden cabinets filled with beautiful fine china and decorative plates. One contained nothing but china dolls. Sarah was always waiting for me and as soon as I arrived she would say, 'Sit down, my friend. Now you just get your cards out and tell me what's going on in my life while I make us both a cup of coffee!'

Her living-room was dominated by a large fireplace. Photos of Andrew in his helicopter pilot's uniform, of their wedding, of her father and several of Beatrice and Eugenie, covered the desktop.

It was at Buckingham Palace that I first met Andrew. I was giving Sarah a reading when he bounded into the room from his adjoining study and greeted me with a crushing handshake. 'It's so nice to meet you at last, Sarah has told me all about you,' he said in his deep, booming voice. His appearance gave no hint that anything was wrong with his marriage and I guessed he could have little or no idea of his wife's true feelings towards him or of her love for another man. He was casually dressed in an open-necked shirt and seemed far less stuffy than I had imagined he would be. The three of us chatted for a couple of minutes before Andrew said he must dash as he had work to do and kissed Sarah on the cheek as he left the room. 'Your husband is a very handsome man,' I said with a smile. 'Oh, Vasso, don't,' Sarah quickly responded, not wanting to linger on my first impressions of the man to whom she was being unfaithful.

Sarah rarely discussed Andrew's previous girlfriends but, on one occasion, she became very jealous during a concert at Sunninghill Park because she believed that Andrew had flirted with a pretty foreign harpist. She tried to hide her feelings, but she was angry that Andrew had dared to look at another woman when he was in her company. She told me there had been a furious row when the guests had left. 'I don't know what he thought he was playing at,' she said. 'He made himself look quite ridiculous.' I found it funny that Sarah was chastising her husband for admiring another woman while she was having an affair under his nose, and I asked if she was maybe just a little jealous. 'No, no, of course not,' Sarah said, before adding, 'Well, maybe just a little bit. She was a very attractive girl.'

....................*

I met Andrew again on my first visit to Sunninghill Park. He was standing just inside the front door as the butler let me in. 'Hello, Vasso, do come upstairs,' he said. 'Sarah's been looking forward to seeing you.'

We walked past the police security room by the front door and Andrew led me up a beautiful, curved staircase to a large first-floor living-room that overlooked the gardens. All around the room — on the mantelpiece, tables and the many bookshelves — were photographs of Andrew, Sarah and the children. Several books featuring illustrations by famous Greek artists caught my eye and, as Sarah came into the room and greeted me with a hug, I said, 'I see you have very good taste!' She laughed and told me how much she adored books on art, adding, to humour me, 'Especially Greek art!'

Pink and red roses had been stencilled on to the walls at either side of the fireplace and above the rail from which hung the rich, cream-coloured curtains. A large wicker basket was filled with logs for the open fire, which was merrily crackling away.

Although the room was large it felt warm, comfortable and lived in. 'You have a lovely home,' I told Sarah. Smiling, she said, 'Thank you, Vasso, it's so good of you to drive all this way to see me.' Then she shooed Andrew out of the room, saying, 'Husband, out! You can leave us in peace for a little while; we've got a lot of things to talk about.'

Poor Andrew. Little did he know that it was the other man in her life, his rival in love, that Sarah wanted to discuss. He seemed such a warm and friendly man, totally oblivious to Sarah's affair with Steven, and I couldn't help feeling sorry for him.

But Sarah did not seem to be bothered that she was discussing her lover while her husband went about his work in another part of the house. 'Don't worry about Andrew, he's a big boy, he'll be all right,' she said dismissively. 'Now come on, Vasso, concentrate and tell me about Steven; what do you see in the cards for us?'

..................*

Usually, when I visited Sunninghill Park, I would stay for three or four hours. The children were always there and Beatrice would come running in and out of the room, asking her mother a thousand and one questions before rushing off to see her nanny in another room. 'Aren't they sweet?' Sarah would say to me. 'Beatrice is like this all day, from the moment she wakes up until the moment she goes to sleep. I don't know where she gets all her energy. I know I could certainly use some of it.' Sometimes Beatrice would sit on my knee and ask why I was visiting her mamma, which always made Sarah laugh. 'Vasso's a very good friend of mine,' she would tell her; 'She's helping mamma sort out some problems.'

The house, standing in four acres of land near Windsor Great Park, was often criticised in the Press for being too modern and ugly. It was dubbed 'South York' because of its resemblance to a Dallas-style fortress, surrounded by eight-foot high walls. But, no matter what one thought of its façade, inside it was magnificent and no expense had been spared. Huge vases of flowers in every room kept the house smelling clean and fresh. 'Flowers are my weakness, Vasso, I just can't resist them,' Sarah would tell me. Wherever she was, at home or abroad, she would insist on flowers in every room.

Once, as I drove to Sunninghill Park, I got hopelessly lost in the roads leading to the estate. Just as I had given up all hope of ever finding the house, a car suddenly appeared behind me flashing its lights and furiously beeping its horn. I was very flustered and pulled over to let it pass but, instead, it stopped behind me and, to my amazement, Andrew got out of the passenger's seat. 'Where have you been, Vasso?' he said, as I wound down the window. 'Sarah was getting frantic with worry so she sent me out to find you. She thought something awful must have happened. I think you had better follow me back to the house!' Andrew was so charming and I was grateful to him. 'You are very kind, but please don't drive too fast or I'm sure to get lost again,' I told him.

As we pulled up outside the house, Andrew dashed inside and I heard him yelling to Sarah that everything was fine, I had simply got lost. Sarah greeted me at the door: 'We were worried something had happened to you, it's such a relief to see that you are all right. You've driven here before — how did you get so lost?' I had no idea where I had gone wrong and told Sarah all I needed now was a strong cup of coffee.

..................*

During our many long conversations, Sarah would often tell me how she first began to wonder if her marriage had been a huge mistake just twenty-four hours after she had made her wedding vows. She began to panic at what she had let herself in for and wondered if she would really be able to cope with living within the confines of the Royal Family, knowing that her every move would be noted by Palace courtiers and her every public and private appearance reported in the Press. She realised for the first time that her life would never again be her own, and it terrified her.

She also began to see Andrew in a new light, realising that he was not in a position to stand up to other, more senior, members of his family or even to the palace officials who played such a key role in the running of all their lives. He went with the flow, and did as he was told. Sarah, however, was a strong-willed woman, used to doing what *she* wanted to do. Life was never going to be the same again and the pre-marital briefings on life within the Royal Family, which she had listened to so glibly, began to dawn on her. She had entered royal life determined not to be intimidated by the palace machine or swamped by protocol. She had assured her family and friends that they would not be frozen out simply because she had joined the world's most famous family. However, she soon realised that she was fighting a losing battle.

Whatever the Palace machine told Andrew to do, he did. If he was told to turn up at an event with Sarah, he insisted they do so, no matter how she was feeling.

During those early, difficult days experienced by so many newly-weds, Sarah was never consulted and the more it happened, the more she came to resent it.

Whenever Sarah suggested that they do something different, so they could be alone for a few, precious hours, Andrew would have none of it. 'You knew it would be like this, you'll just have to accept it,' he would tell her. This always left Sarah feeling upset. 'I just wished he could have been a little more understanding,' Sarah said. 'If only he had bought me flowers or done something to show he loved me, but it never happened. I loved him so much in those early days, but it was all so one-sided.'

She explained how the first cracks had begun to appear in their marriage during the late summer months of 1988, not long after the birth of her first daughter, Beatrice. By and large, Sarah had enjoyed the first two years of married life and — although she was not spending anywhere near as much time with Andrew as she would have liked — she was happy because they shared the same sense of fun and spirit, which friends hoped would bind them together for ever.

After the birth of Beatrice, Sarah had been deeply hurt by media criticism of her leaving her newborn baby when she travelled to Australia to join Andrew, who was there on tour. The newspaper attacks were all the more hurtful because she had desperately wanted to take Beatrice with her, but had been persuaded by Andrew and other members of the Royal Household that it would be better to leave the child at home. Although Andrew told her to ignore the criticism and not to worry about the newspaper stories, Sarah tried to defend herself publicly by saying: 'I thought it was more important to be with my husband. I'm very old-fashioned, but he came first.' The truth was that Sarah should have followed Andrew's advice and said nothing. By fighting back, she attracted even more scrutiny. Staying silent may have been the Royal Family's way but, unfortunately, it was not Sarah's way. She had been used to speaking up and saying exactly what she thought. 'I tried very hard, but whatever I did or said seemed to be wrong. I never seemed to be able to do anything right. It was all so demoralising.'

This led to the first undercurrent of public hostility towards Sarah, who was left feeling angry at the lack of support from both her husband and from Buckingham Palace, whose officials did little or nothing to defend her.

On her return from Australia, and still suffering from post-natal depression, she was left to brood on the stinging Press attacks. Sarah, who desperately wanted to be loved by everyone, was deeply hurt at being publicly criticised. She was not used to it and she would lie awake at night for hours, often with tears streaming down her face, wondering how she could put things right. She was sure that Andrew would look after her and protect her reputation but, as the weeks passed, she became increasingly depressed at the amount of time he spent away from home because of his naval career. She bombarded him with love letters but he seldom, if ever, replied and her feelings of neglect grew almost daily. 'You know, Vasso, I'd write to him almost every day and eagerly await the post for his return letters but they never came,' she told me. 'I was missing him madly and couldn't understand why he couldn't spare the time to let me know what he was up to. I was interested to know how he was getting on and for him to write back and say how much he was missing me. But he never did. It was so depressing.'

With Andrew away, the social whirl of high-society parties and glittering film premières that Sarah so enjoyed quickly diminished. She felt that the promises they had made about always being there for each other had been broken. She felt terribly alone and vulnerable. 'I just didn't really understand what I was letting myself in for,' Sarah told me. 'Suddenly, everything I did and everything I said was reported in the papers. The Press commented on the way I looked, what I was wearing and even my weight. It was as if everyone had a right to know my every move. It was terrifying.' To all intents and purposes, she was living the life of a lonely single parent, a million miles away from the wedded bliss she had dreamed of.

When Andrew was asked about the amount of time they spent apart, he responded: 'I don't like it. Full stop.'

CHAPTER FIVE
HOUSTON, TEXAS

In November 1989, Sarah, bored and feeling unloved, and five months pregnant with her second daughter, accepted an invitation to fly to Houston, Texas, to attend a British festival. It was a trip that would have a most profound effect on her life, for it was there that she first met and fell for the charms of the wealthy and extremely handsome bachelor Steven Wyatt. Steven, who was 35, was rarely seen without a beautiful girl on his arm, but he had just ended a three-year affair with the model Denice Lewis, having finished with her on Christmas Eve in the ski resort of Aspen. He was a free agent again and he caught Sarah's eye immediately.

She felt like a teenager falling in love as Steven gently flirted with her during an opera and late-night ball they had both attended. Sarah would later tell me that she was completely bowled over by his easy-going manner and, in particular, his attentiveness. He was amusing and made her laugh, and it was clear to those closest to them that the pair hit it off straight away.

Sarah quickly discovered that they shared similar views on a wide range of issues and there was never a shortage of things to talk about. Steven's father, Oscar, invited her to the family's luxurious ranch near Rio Grande and she was impressed with the friendliness with which she was welcomed. Sarah, who had qualified as a helicopter pilot to impress Andrew, relished the opportunity of taking the controls of the family helicopter as she was given a guided tour of the Wyatt's 20,000-acre property. The friendship distracted her from the sad state of her marriage: Steven was someone she enjoyed being with and she felt sure the feelings were mutual. No doubt he was impressed at landing such a great catch, a member of Britain's Royal Family, even if it was somewhat unfortunate that she was already married. 'He was so kind to me in those early days,' Sarah recalled. 'I knew I was falling in love with him, but there was nothing I could do to stop myself.'

The trip lasted only six days, but it was long enough for Sarah to fall totally under his spell. Steven was like a breath of fresh air, putting the wind back into her deflated sails. He gave her a new zest for life. It was all so sudden, so exciting and new, that Sarah fell in love within a few short days.

She would later tell me that when she first met Steven, she was still in love with Andrew, despite her feelings of loneliness and neglect. But within weeks of meeting her new companion, her feelings towards her husband began to change. Suddenly, there was a new man on the scene offering her the love and warmth she craved.

From that time, the sexual side of her relationship with Andrew began to die. 'I just never had the urge to sleep with Andrew again after Steven,' she told me. 'If anything, I began to look on Andrew as a big brother. If he was there, he was there, if he wasn't, he wasn't. It was as simple as that.'

She constantly talked to Diana and a few other close friends about leaving Andrew and getting a divorce, so that she could escape from 'the system' she so hated. 'I just didn't know what to do,' she told me. 'I wanted to be free, to get a divorce and escape the mess my life had become. I couldn't stand the way they treated me or the way Andrew paid so little attention to me. It was no life for anyone.'

Over the following months, her relationship with Steven intensified. In December, he flew to England and was one of the guests at a high-society shooting party that gathered at the Yorkshire home of Charles and Maggie Wyvill, wealthy members of the British aristocracy. Sarah appeared at the dinner party, unexpectedly stayed the night and next morning, still wearing her dark-blue velvet evening dress, posed for pictures with other members of the party. It did not go unnoticed that she chose to sit at the feet of a certain Steven Wyatt.

To their American neighbours, it may have seemed prestigious to be so closely linked to the Royal Family but to Steven's mother, Lynn, the relationship spelt nothing but trouble. She warned him of the damage that such a scandal would do to the family name and advised him to cool the affair. She genuinely liked Sarah and the two women got on well, but Lynn was worried that her son would be made to look the villain and leave her out of favour with the Queen. Sarah told me that Lynn also strongly disapproved of her son having an affair with a married woman and repeatedly warned him it would end in tears.

Although Andrew was not primarily to blame for the breakdown of their marriage, I was angry with him for not being around more when Sarah most needed him. When she was pregnant and feeling most sensitive, he buried himself in his work as if that was the main thing that mattered. Had he spent more time with his wife, made a fuss of her every now and then and told her how much he loved her, which he obviously did, Sarah might never have gone to Houston and never met Steven. I felt Andrew didn't support her enough and deserves to take some of the blame for the failure of the marriage. Even when he did come home from his naval duties, Sarah told me he would spend most of his time slumped in front of the television watching videos or playing golf. He was not putting enough into the relationship and gradually Sarah was slipping further and further away from him. It was as if he had given up on their marriage without ever really giving it a chance and it saddened me a great deal.

One close friend of Sarah's said at the time: 'I wish I could have knocked some sense into Andrew, he seemed so totally oblivious to the fact that he was losing Sarah. He just switched off and didn't want to know. Whenever I spoke to her about it, she just shrugged her shoulders and told me not to worry. She said trying to speak to Andrew would be a waste of time. She said if he couldn't be bothered to make an effort, then neither could she.'

..................*

Eugenie, sixth in line to the throne, was born at London's Portland Hospital on the evening of 23 March, 1990, by caesarean section, and weighed in at just over seven pounds. Andrew had barely made it to the hospital in time for the birth after driving himself from Devonport, the Plymouth naval base where his frigate *Cambeltown* was based.

To most of the world, it was the latest chapter of the fairytale. Andrew bounded from the hospital saying everything had gone very well and both mother and baby were doing fine. 'I'll be back tomorrow,' he said with a cheery smile.

But to Sarah, who was then 30 years old, the birth came at one of the most traumatic periods of her life. The man she was in love with, the man she spent hours chatting to on the phone every day, the man she desperately wanted at her bedside was not her husband, the father of her child. It was Steven, and she knew he couldn't be there. She was in emotional turmoil and hopelessly confused as she tried to put on a happy and united front with Andrew, whom she felt had not shown sufficient concern during the difficult months of her pregnancy. It upset her deeply that Andrew had not been around to see Beatrice hesitantly take her first few steps or utter her first words, and now she felt it was going to happen all over again with Eugenie — although that was not her main concern. As she lay in her hospital bed recovering from the birth, she spent hours fretting over Steven, wondering if his feelings for her would still be as strong now that she had a second daughter. She was terrified that he would want nothing more to do with her and call the whole thing off. All the stress and the worrying about whether things would work out for the best left Sarah an emotional wreck.

A string of visitors arrived to see the latest addition to the Royal Family, but Sarah was most pleased to see her sister Jane and sister-in-law Diana, who stayed for more than an hour. Diana was probably one of the few people who understood exactly what her close friend was going through; she knew of the affair with Steven and of Sarah's inner turmoil.

A week after leaving hospital, Sarah held Eugenie in her arms as she posed for an official photograph with Andrew and Beatrice — a depiction of the perfect family. Andrew, with his elder daughter sitting on his knee, and Sarah, cradling her newborn child, looked like any other proud parents. To the millions who looked at the photo there was not the slightest hint that anything could possibly be wrong. No one could possibly have imagined that the smiling mother was desperately in love with another man. Andrew quickly disappeared back to his naval base and Sarah was once again alone.

It would not be long before the warning bells would begin to ring within Royal circles. Just five short weeks after Eugenie's birth, on 2 May, 1990, Sarah slipped out of the country for a holiday in Morocco and an emotional reunion with the love of her life. Sarah later told me that she had been a bag of nerves when she rang Steven for the first time after the birth, although she needn't have worried. He assured her that he was still madly in love with her and couldn't wait to hold her in his arms. He borrowed his father's private jet and whisked Sarah away for a romantic holiday in the sun. The full impact of that trip would not be felt for some time, but it would come back to haunt her.

Recalling the trip Sarah told me, 'I just had to get away. Steven was desperate to see me and a trip abroad was the only way we could be assured of being alone. It was a wonderful holiday, Steven was so warm and considerate I didn't miss Andrew at all. He came back briefly for the birth but then he was gone again, back to his bloody work. Steven understood how I was feeling. He knew I was totally drained after Eugenie's birth and he didn't make any demands on me. He was happy doing what I wanted to do. I felt we were both hopelessly in love with each other. Everything seemed too good to be true.' Which, of course, it was.

After Eugenie's birth, Sarah was only ever happy and relaxed when she was with Steven. She told me they chatted away like a couple of young lovers. 'He says I'm wonderful and beautiful, it's music to my ears,' she said with a smile. She also admitted that they made love whenever they had the opportunity. She would often tell me, 'You wouldn't believe the night I've had. Steven is such a wonderful lover. We made love over and over again. We hardly slept, but I feel so alive, so invigorated. I have never experienced anything quite like it.'

She told me that Steven was very proud of his body

and regularly worked out to keep himself in trim. He believed his daily routine of yoga enhanced his love-making and there were certainly never any complaints from Sarah. Once, when Steven had visited her at Sunninghill Park while Andrew was away, they had gone for a midnight stroll through the vast gardens. 'It had been such a lovely evening,' she said. 'We stopped to kiss on the little bridge at the bottom of the gardens and got a bit carried away. We ended up making love under the stars!' she told me. 'Can you imagine if someone had seen us, Vasso? Aren't I terrible?'

She seemed so happy and in love, but it worried me that she was still a married woman, with two little girls who were grand-daughters of the Queen, and I knew that the relationship spelt nothing but trouble.

I told her of my concerns and warned her to be careful that she didn't get hurt or make a fool of herself. But I knew that it went in one ear and out the other, as Sarah said, 'Just you stop worrying and fetch those cards. Tell me what's going to happen and I don't want any bad news. Tell me everything's going to be all right.'

Sarah's friendship with Steven was becoming intense and she seemed to be taking more and more risks of being seen in public with him. She would ask me what she should do during her frequent late-night phone calls, but I told her, 'You are a very strong girl and you know you will make up your own mind no matter what anyone tells you. You must not rush into anything, you have your whole life ahead of you, so you must consider what to do very carefully.'

I believed she would be much better off with Andrew and told her so. 'You must sit down together and talk about your problems,' I told her. 'How else can you expect him to know what you are going through?' I begged her not to give up on Andrew, for I could see in the cards that they still had a future together. I told her there would soon come a time when he would realise what a fool he had been in neglecting her and treating her so badly and would do everything he could to win back her love. But it wasn't what Sarah wanted to hear. I would spend hours reading the cards for Sarah, but all she really wanted to know about was Steven.

It went on like this for months, until one day Sarah told me, 'It's no use, Vasso, I'm at the end of my tether. I've tried talking to Andrew, but he doesn't want to listen. I've decided to see the Queen and tell her I want a separation. I know she will try to stop me, but I've made up my mind. I cannot carry on like this. Being torn apart like this is destroying me.' Again, I begged her to be careful and not to throw away all she had, but I knew I was wasting my breath. She had made up her mind and there was nothing I or anyone else could do to change it. It was now only a matter of time.

Sarah would escape for foreign holidays with

Steven whenever she could, always doing her best to slip out of the country unnoticed, although everyone in the royal circle knew, through the Buckingham Palace grapevine, exactly where she was going and what she was up to. Sometimes, Sarah and Steven would flee to Portugal to stay at a villa owned by friends. It was a discreet hideaway where they felt totally relaxed and out of sight of prying eyes. Whenever she was away she would ring me, usually late at night, to say what she had been up to and to ask for a reading over the telephone. 'It's so fantastic, it's like a whole new life,' she would tell me. 'I feel so in love again and it's a wonderful feeling.' I would often warn Sarah that there were dark clouds on the horizon, but she didn't want to know about them. She wanted nothing to get in the way of her happiness.

In August 1990, while Andrew was away, she arranged a dinner at Buckingham Palace for an Iraqi oil minister with whom Steven was keen to clinch a business deal. Later that night, the Duchess took Steven to a top London nightclub, where they seemed to be inseparable. Later, newspapers claimed that Steven had astonished their host, the then Conservative Party treasurer Lord McAlpine, by refusing to sit at another table and telling him, 'Mah woman and I sit together.' It was terribly indiscreet of them, but Sarah seemed past caring. 'We had a great night — let them say what they want,' she said.

Later that year, in December, she was even foolish enough to invite Steven as her special guest to a Buckingham Palace ball celebrating the birthdays of the Queen Mother, who was 90, Princess Margaret, who was 60, Princess Anne, who was 40 ... and her own husband, who was 30. She was playing a dangerous game that ultimately could only end in tears.

Sarah was well aware of Palace disapproval of her association with Steven, as she had been advised on more than one occasion to cool her relationship with the good-looking oilman. People were beginning to talk and the Press was having a field day. Sarah and Steven would regularly share intimate candle-lit dinners together, usually choosing discreet Italian restaurants. To try to avoid arousing suspicion, they would take along a mutual girlfriend, often a Portuguese lady or an American actress friend of Steven's, but the cover fooled few people who saw them together. On other occasions, they would meet for games of tennis at the Royal Berkshire Racquets Club at Bracknell, just a stone's throw from Sarah's marital home. They would never play together, but Steven would usually be found watching from the spectators' benches. Gary Drake, Sarah's personal coach, revealed, 'Sarah and Steven are very good friends. They like it here because the atmosphere is friendly and nobody bothers them. Nobody takes any notice of them. They both enjoy each other's company. They share the same sense of humour and laugh a lot.'

Sarah later told me, 'Everyone kept telling me that I shouldn't see Steven, but as far as I was concerned it was none of their business. I don't know who the hell these people think they are. It's as if they feel they can pick and choose my friends for me. No one is really bothered about me, all they care about is being seen to do the right thing.'

The growing rumours of Sarah's friendship with Steven had blackened Andrew's mood. But, instead of trying to tackle the problem, he buried himself even deeper in his work. 'He's given up, he doesn't care, so why should I?' Sarah would say. They rarely saw each other and even when they did, few words were spoken. Perhaps if he had tried to talk to Sarah during those troubled times, he could have done something to salvage the marriage, but either he simply couldn't be bothered or he hoped that by ignoring the situation it would go away. I suspected it was the latter and that his main problem was his inability to communicate with Sarah without it ending in a blazing row. As a naval officer, he was used to dealing with men who were far less complicated and gave him few problems because they always obeyed his commands and never answered back. The same could never be said of Sarah.

So Andrew tried to pretend that the rumours couldn't be true. To me, he seemed like an ostrich burying his head in the sand. 'Why don't you try to talk to Andrew?' I would often ask her. But she would respond, 'Oh, it's too late for that and anyway, I'd be wasting my breath. He's past caring and so am I.' I read that during 1990, Sarah and Andrew had spent just 42 nights together and asked her if that was true. 'Yes it is, Vasso,' she told me. 'It's dreadful, but I think it says it all really.'

Sarah was constantly searching for love and when it didn't come from Andrew, it is not surprising that she sought it elsewhere. Andrew didn't seem to appreciate fully his responsibility to her and the children. To him it was just work, work, work. He failed to understand that Sarah was a very insecure young woman who needed to be told she was loved and wanted. She worried about everything, trusted no one and, although she always gave the impression of being cheerful and happy when she was with Steven, deep down she always felt that the walls of her life were about to come tumbling down. 'I'm so happy, although I know it can't last, but why not? Why is life so unfair?' she would ask. Her insecurity stretched back to her school days when teachers revealed she would go out of her way to win the affection of classmates. I'm sure this was because she had been left deeply scarred by the breakdown of her parents' marriage. At school, where she was a weekly boarder, she always wanted to be the centre of attention, often playing the classroom jester in her bid to win friends and ensure that everyone would like her. In her adult life, little had changed.

Sarah told me that she had been so deeply in love with Andrew during the early days of their romance. Both wanted a big family and were keen to have a son, a subject they even discussed, surprisingly, after Eugenie's birth. Sarah loved children and idolised her daughters. Nothing was ever too much trouble as far as they were concerned. Naturally, the girls had nannies but Sarah was always there for them when they needed her. She knew from her own experience what it was like not to have a mother around and she was determined never to inflict that trauma on her own daughters. 'My babies are the most important thing in the world to me. I will never let anything come between us.'

Whenever I visited her I could see for myself how much she doted and fussed over them, reading them stories and letting Beatrice brush her long red hair. Apart from anything else, Sarah was very lonely and the girls were great company for her. She was determined not to send them to school at too early an age, although she knew she would be under pressure to do whatever the Family considered right. 'I think home life is very important,' she said. 'I've got two lovely girls and what's the point of sending them to school for months on end?' Whenever possible, she took the girls on her travels believing it was good for them to experience new cultures and broaden their horizons.

To Sarah, the tongue-wagging about her relationship with Steven was water off a duck's back. No one would tell her what to do. 'Who do they think they are?' she would ask me. 'I'm having fun and I'll do what I want.' But it was almost as if she was on self-destruct. Nothing could stop Sarah in her quest for happiness. She believed Andrew had given up on their marriage so what did she care. Of course, he dearly loved their daughters but the spark that had first lit their relationship and led to the magnificent wedding at Westminster Abbey on 23 July, 1986, had all but fizzled out.

Steven, on the other hand, was charming, witty and, above all, attentive. He made her feel wanted and that was something Sarah desperately needed and craved. 'Oh, Vasso, Vasso what should I do?' she would ask me. 'I love Steven, but will we ever be allowed to be together?'

Whenever we did a reading, Sarah would quiz me about him: 'Tell me what the future holds for our relationship. Steven is worried about his business, do you think he is going to be successful?' Time after time, I warned Sarah to be careful for although I could see that Steven's business dealings were going to be a success, his private life with her was another matter. 'There are always other women around him,' I warned. 'You must be careful, my baby, I don't want to see you get hurt.' Sarah would guardedly respond, 'But Steven says he loves me and wants to marry me. He says he wants us to be together for the rest of our days. He keeps telling me everything is going to be all right and that I shouldn't worry.'

On a number of occasions Sarah challenged him about reports of his affairs with other women, but he always denied there was anyone else in his life. 'You mustn't believe everything you read in the newspapers,' he told her. 'You know you're the only one for me.' And Sarah foolishly believed him because she wanted to believe him, pushing any thoughts that he might be seeing someone else to the back of her mind.

Although she would always plead for my advice in these situations, deep down I knew that whatever I told her, she would follow her own heart and do as she wanted. It was a whirlwind romance gathering momentum at such a speed that it frightened me. 'Please be careful,' I begged her. Every phone call and every visit showed me that her feelings were growing stronger day by day. It was always 'Steven said this' or 'Steven said that'. She was head over heels in love with him and she dreamed that once divorced, she and Steven would settle down and become man and wife. 'Steven is everything that Andrew's not,' Sarah told me. 'He's mature, warm and considerate. We are so ideally suited and I know he loves me as much as I do him because he rings me every day to tell me. We're soulmates, Vasso, we really are.' She also confided that Steven loved her daughters and they looked on him as a favourite uncle. 'Steven really loves children and the girls think he's great. But I don't think Andrew would be too pleased if he found out quite how close they were. He'd probably hit the roof!'

Whenever Steven was in London, Sarah would arrange to meet him at the luxury flat he rented for £2,400 a month in Cadogan Square, Knightsbridge. It was the only place where they could be totally alone and Sarah always longed for his next visit. She told me she was terrified of being spotted entering the building and of the Press learning of her secret visits so, whenever she went, she would disguise herself by wearing a wig or wrapping a scarf over her head to hide her distinctive red hair. She would sneak out in the early hours of the morning when there was no one around.

As she lay in Steven's strong arms, she dreamt of starting a new life with him in the USA. But Sarah knew she would never be allowed to take the girls to live abroad and that only added to her despair. 'How am I ever going to get myself out of this hopeless mess?' she asked me.

One minute she would appear as if she hadn't a care in the world, the next she would be in floods of tears. She was in a terrible state and knew there no easy way out. Whenever she was depressed she would ring and ask for a reading and if she saw a glimmer of hope in the cards, her spirits would again be lifted.

It was impossible not to like Steven. He was polite and very charming, especially with the ladies, but that was one of the reasons why I knew there was no long-term future for him and Sarah.

I had often warned Sarah through my readings that I sensed there were other women in his life. One face in particular kept cropping up and I did my best to warn Sarah that there was another woman very close to him. Before they met, he had a reputation as a playboy and I was convinced that he was seeing other women behind Sarah's back as, over the months, he grew bored of being constantly hounded by the Press. Initially, I think he had enjoyed the notoriety of being linked with an English Duchess, but the fact that she was married was a complication that he decided he could do without.

On several occasions he came to visit me alone at my Islington home. Steven, like Sarah, had a deep belief in faith healers and the powers of the pyramids. He slept with a brass pyramid hanging over his bed because he believed it had mystical healing powers that could cleanse and heal his soul. Every morning, after rising at 5.30 a.m., he would sit meditating for an hour and undergo a gruelling yoga regime.

The first time Steven came to see me, he booked an appointment without letting on who he was. I answered the door to a well-built, but not particularly tall man, with a strong American accent who held out his hand and said, 'Hi, I'm Steven, it's good of you to see me.' He was wearing a long, dark, very expensive overcoat and clutching a large briefcase that appeared to be bursting at the seams. Under the coat he wore a huge pair of baggy trousers, which made me laugh to myself, and a casual open-necked shirt. 'You've been recommended by a very close friend of mine,' he told me. 'I've got a lot of things I want to discuss with you; I sure hope you're going to be able to help me.'

Leading him upstairs to my healing room and sitting down opposite him, I saw a handsome young man in his mid-30s, with a mass of dark wavy hair, a strong jaw and piercing blue eyes. When he spoke, it was slowly and confidently. It was obvious to me from that first meeting that for him work came first. He told me he was very close to clinching a business deal and wanted to know if he was going to be successful. Steven was straight-talking and positive and I had little doubt that he would be a success and I told him so. But he seemed rather reluctant to discuss his private life on that first meeting and, when I told him I could see many beautiful women in his life, it seemed to cause him some embarrassment. He left after nearly an hour, never once mentioning that he was the new man in the life of the Duchess of York, although I had, of course, recognised him from the photograph Sarah had shown me.

Sarah rang later to ask what I thought of the man who had stolen her heart. 'He is very handsome,' I told her. 'Yes, yes, he is, isn't he, Vasso? Even better than in the photograph,' she gushed. 'Did you like him? Tell me what you thought of him. Do you think we are right for each other?' Sarah wanted to know if he had mentioned her but I said he seemed far more interested in his business dealings, which made her laugh. 'His business is so important to him,' Sarah said. 'He feels as if he's got so much to prove to his family. He desperately wants to be a success, I'm sure he will be.'

Sarah told me that Steven was always trying to close oil deals, to become a wealthy man like his father, for although his family was worth millions, Sarah told me that he was not yet rich in his own right. 'Steven always worries a great deal about his business deals, but I love him so much I wouldn't care if he didn't have a penny to his name,' she said. 'All that matters is being with him.'

On his next visit, Steven told me that he had not mentioned Sarah's name as he wanted to be discreet but also because Sarah had begged him not to as she was intrigued to know what I would tell him. He said he was very much in love with Sarah and that she was a very special lady, but the fact that he was not wealthy in his own right troubled him. 'I must have enough money to ensure I can look after Sarah and the girls,' he told me. 'I want the best for all of them.'

He rang several times and asked for a reading over the telephone. On each occasion, he told me how much he loved and adored Sarah and how he hoped that one day they could make a life of their own together, with Sarah as his wife. I questioned Steven about another woman I could see in the cards, but he laughed it off, saying Sarah was the only one for him. I was not convinced.

Even in those early days, Sarah worried about her own financial situation for she knew she was far too reckless with money. In the early years as a member of the Royal Family, it was spend, spend, spend, as she lived the good life to the full. Occasionally she would be jolted by a bank statement, the figures of her wild extravagances leaping out at her in black and white. But she would quickly lock them away in a drawer and block her worries out of her mind, believing, like a child, that everything would be all right in the end.

Sarah told me that Steven often found himself strapped for 'ready cash' and she would usually pay when they went out together. A number of times when he was experiencing 'cash flow' problems, she had lent him large sums of money to tide him over. She doubted if she would ever see the money again, but it didn't seem to worry her. 'I'll help him out however I can,' she said. 'Everyone needs a helping hand in life and I know he's going to be a great success.'

During one of Steven's visits, he told me that he

was very close to winning an important contract, a huge oil deal with an African country. Stupidly, I let slip that one of my clients and long-time friends was Chief Moshood Abiola, who was strongly tipped to win the forthcoming presidential elections in oil-rich Nigeria.

Steven's eyes lit up immediately and he asked if there was any way I could arrange an introduction. The millionaire chief was already a powerful politician, and Steven must have been well aware of the influence he would have over the control of oil exportation if elected president. A few days later, he rang to say that he had arranged for me to meet one of his business associates in Chelsea and I, somewhat reluctantly, agreed to attend the meeting after he told me he had arranged for Sarah to meet me outside the man's offices. His associate, an American who already had business interests in Nigeria and offices in Lagos, was intrigued to know how I knew the chief and suggested that I arrange a meeting and give him Abiola's personal telephone number, which I refused to do. 'You have no idea how important this is,' the man argued; 'If we can pull off a deal with the Nigerians, it would be worth £50,000 to you every month. You *must* arrange a meeting for me.'

I had never met this man before and scoffed at his promises but, because I was with Sarah, who I knew was there only for Steven, I told him that I would see what I could do. Sarah encouraged me to help him, because it would also help Steven. However, I was deeply wary of the man.

Over the next few weeks, he rang me five or six times while I was visiting friends in Cyprus, having persuaded Sarah to give him my telephone number. I told him he must be patient and wait and I would raise the matter when I visited Nigeria in a few months' time. But he was impatient, saying the business wouldn't wait and I must make the contact now or it would be too late. 'I don't care if you are going to Nigeria, you must arrange a meeting for me now,' he demanded. If that was the case, then so be it, I told him. There was nothing he could say or do to make me change my mind.

I was furious and, on my return to the UK, rang Sarah to tell her how rude the man had been and that I had no intention of helping him. Realising how angry I was, she apologised for giving him my number and assured me that she would pass on the message that I was unable to help. Despite this, he rang several times over the next few weeks before finally giving me up as a lost cause.

My association with Nigeria stretched back to 1980 when the wife of a Nigerian chief, who had regularly visited me for readings, had an operation in London. As she had no family living in London, I visited her every day, brought her flowers and ensured she had all she needed. After she had made a full recovery and returned to Nigeria, she sent me an air ticket and urged me to visit her so that she could thank me for all I had done. It was through her that I was introduced to the families of a number of the country's most influential politicians, including Chief Abiola. Sadly, the chief was put under house arrest in June 1993 when the elections were annulled by the military-backed interim government after it became apparent that Abiola would be the clear winner. The elections had been declared free and fair by international observers but, despite worldwide condemnation at the *coup d'état*, the chief remains under house arrest and in constant fear for his life to this day.

CHAPTER SIX
MAJOR RON AND LESLEY PLAYER

Sarah encouraged her father, Major Ronald Ferguson, to visit me. On his first visit, he drove himself to my home in his maroon BMW, arriving an hour and a half early for the appointment. When he pulled up outside, he rang me on his mobile telephone, apologising profusely and asking if I could possibly see him a little early as he had a business meeting later in the day. When he came into the house, he introduced himself as 'Lady's father' and thanked me for seeing him at such short notice.

A tall, imposing man, with a deep, military-sounding voice and a firm handshake, he was smartly dressed in a blue, double-breasted blazer with a silk handkerchief poking out of his top pocket. The creases in his grey trousers were razor sharp, but I did notice that his shoes were old and worn and looked as if they had seen better days. There was even a small hole in one of the heels. He had enormous bushy ginger eyebrows and a worried frown on his face suggested that he had the troubles of the world on his rather slumped shoulders. As I made him a cup of coffee, he told me that he had some problems he would like to discuss and asked if I would do a reading for him. 'I've come to see if you really are as wonderful as that daughter of mine keeps telling me you are,' he said.

Once inside my healing room, he openly admitted that he was having an affair and asked if I could tell him how things would work out. He still loved his wife a great deal, although his marriage had gone somewhat stale, but was totally smitten by this new, younger and very attractive woman who had come into his life 'as if by a miracle', making him feel ten years younger. 'I know you probably think I'm being an old fool, but I'm desperately in love with her,' he told me. 'Her name's Lesley. She makes me feel so young again. She's an incredible girl, full of life and with the most wonderful smile I've ever seen. Just thinking about her lifts my spirits.'

He explained that they had met when she turned to him for advice on organising a polo tournament 'and the relationship just sort of developed from there'. At the time, he was the sponsorships' director at the Royal County of Berkshire Polo Club and he had been Prince Charles' polo manager for 21 years. The Major was in a bit of a state and doubted whether he would ever be able to leave his wife, but at the same time he was terrified of losing Lesley. 'In other words, you want to have your cake and eat it!' I said, to which he replied, 'Yes, I suppose that's about right, really. I know I'm probably making a ridiculous fool of myself, but I can't get Lesley out of my mind.' Studying the cards, I could see that the older of the two women would be more prominent in his life in later years and I told him that his wife would stick by him because she obviously loved him a great deal. I told him that, although it would be difficult, he should try to overcome his infatuation with Lesley, who was 33. Otherwise, his troubles would only get worse, not better. 'The longer this affair continues, the harder it will affect you when it ends,' I said. 'You must be realistic: it is an affair and most affairs come to an end. You have a good wife who loves you, do not give up on your marriage because you have too much to lose.'

We talked about Sarah and her affair with Steven, which troubled him a great deal. He believed, as I did, that the relationship was destined for trouble and said he desperately hoped she and Andrew could work out their differences and give their marriage another go. 'I cannot understand what's gone so wrong between them,' he said. 'But I know the sooner she gets this chap Wyatt out of her life the better. If she doesn't, there will be all sorts of problems ahead.' I smiled and told him, 'It is exactly the same for you. Marriage is too precious to give up lightly.' The Major said nothing, but looked down, closing his eyes and clutching his bald forehead in one of his large hands. There was silence for some moments before he looked up, stroked his jaw and replied, 'You've certainly given me a lot to think about.'

He left after two hours saying, 'Thank you so much for seeing me, Vasso. Goodness knows how it will all turn out, but it's so good to be able to discuss openly my situation with someone. I do hope you will let me visit you again soon.'

On another visit he brought Sarah's sister, Jane Makim, who was on holiday from her home in Australia. She was nothing like Sarah, tall and slim but very plain and nowhere near as bubbly or as warm. As I gave her a reading, she told me that she was worried about a battle she was fighting with her ex-husband over their two children and asked how things would work out. There was also a new man in her life and she wanted to know if they would marry and have children of their own. I studied the cards and warned Jane to expect a rough time, for I could see a lot of anguish and grief in the very near future. But, in the long term, I could see a great deal of happiness and believed she would marry this new man and bear him a child, which cheered her up no end.

There was indeed happiness to come for Jane — she

eventually remarried and had a child.

Before long, the Major persuaded Lesley to pay me a visit and, although she spent nearly two hours with me, she never once revealed that she was his new love. I had seen in the cards that there was an older man in her life, but I could also see another man with whom she would fall in love and eventually marry. When Lesley told Ron what I had said to her, he was distraught, 'Oh my God! You're going to meet someone else.' Lesley tried to calm him down by saying that although she was convinced I was a woman of genuine healing powers, he shouldn't worry about my predictions. But Ron dismissed this; like Sarah, he had total confidence in my predictions, and the episode left the already worried Major in an even more disturbed state.

Sarah knew all about the affair and even allowed her father and Lesley to stay together at her marital home. Sarah said she liked Lesley and found her very easy to get along with. She even went as far as creating a 'cover', enabling Lesley to act as her lady-in-waiting on Royal tours so that she could be with the Major.

Sarah later recounted what Lesley had told her father about my prediction, saying, 'Poor old Dad, he's so worried about what you told Lesley that he's got himself into a right old state. He's terrified of losing her.'

It didn't seem to worry her that her father was

having an affair behind his wife's back and I guessed that was probably because it almost exactly mirrored her own situation.

Perhaps the most astonishing twist in the whole sorry saga of the Fergusons' tangled love lives came when Lesley had an affair while still seeing the Major. Attending a society party, she was introduced to a good-looking, tanned American with what she described as a radiant smile — it was Steven Wyatt. Lesley was aware from what the Major had told her that Sarah had a secret lover but, of course, had no idea it was the very man who was now capturing her heart. After agreeing to meet Steven, who wined and dined her at his penthouse flat, she ended up sharing his bed on their first date.

It was only months later, when Lesley told Steven about her work organising a polo tournament with Major Ron Ferguson, with whom she had had an affair, that he realised he was sleeping with both the Duchess and her father's lover and immediately broke off their relationship. The dreadful truth only dawned on Lesley and Ron when she tried to end their affair, saying she had slept with another man, Steven Wyatt, behind his back. Ron was stunned and when he told Lesley who Steven was ... so was she.

CHAPTER SEVEN
THE END OF THE AFFAIR

Andrew had been so wrapped up in his work that he had initially looked on Steven as just another of Sarah's friends. It was only when she had become so indiscreet that the affair was common knowledge to virtually everyone within Royal circles, that word got back to him that there was perhaps more to the friendship than met the eye.

Then, in January 1992, a set of more than a hundred holiday pictures, including several of Sarah and Steven, was found by a window cleaner on top of a wardrobe at his former rented flat. One showed a grinning Steven dangling Beatrice, who was naked, on his knee, another showed Sarah and Steven sitting together on a garden swing. The pictures had been taken on their trip to Morocco two years earlier at the height of their affair, and they proved to be hugely embarrassing.

The exact circumstances of their discovery remains a mystery and it was even suggested there could be a conspiracy to bring about Sarah's downfall, which she believed was a distinct possibility. Andrew had tolerated much, but the pictures of his daughter looking so happy and relaxed with another man infuriated him and he told Sarah during a heated telephone exchange that he could no longer give her his unqualified public support. He was a proud father and he believed that, to the outside world, it would seem as if his place had been taken by another man. The photos certainly showed how comfortable his wife had been in Steven's company and how closely the handsome Texan had been drawn into her life and the lives of their two little daughters.

A friend of his said at the time, 'Andrew is very protective where Bea and Eugenie are concerned. For Sarah to involve them in her friendship with Wyatt was the height of foolishness. Andrew feels guilty enough about not being with his daughters because of his commitment to the Royal Navy. The last thing he would want is for someone like Wyatt to jump in and try to be his stand-in.'

In a tearful confrontation, Sarah confessed. In many ways, she felt relieved that Andrew finally knew. As far as she was concerned, their marriage was all but dead anyway. She had known for some time that she would have to tell him.

Sarah said that Steven was pleased their secret was now out in the open, but I was not so sure that was how he really felt. While she was looking to the future and excitedly making plans for a new life with Steven, I could tell he was starting to get jittery. He may have made promises about wanting to make Sarah his wife, but men say many things during a passionate affair and many promises are later broken. Steven grew even more alarmed after Sarah told him she had seen the Queen and told her she wanted a separation. Everything was moving far too fast for his liking and he started to look for the exit door.

To this day, Sarah finds it difficult to comprehend exactly why Steven suddenly ended their affair. But it had a devastating effect on her. Each time I visited, she would break down and cry, pouring out her heart as she tried to understand why he left her. She would call me in the early hours of the morning, begging for advice on how to sort out the mess that her life had become. 'He has torn me apart and left me an emotional wreck,' she would cry. 'Oh, Vasso, am I never to have peace and happiness in my life?'

Steven had told her that he was becoming increasingly concerned at the publicity about him being part of the break-up of her marriage but Sarah, missing the signs that he really wanted out, simply told him not to worry and that everything would be all right. He even began to make sly remarks about Sarah, saying she was putting on weight, which upset her deeply. 'He didn't mind about my size when I was pregnant,' Sarah told me. 'He said I was beautiful. Why does he have to say these things now? I thought he was the last person in the world who would say something like that.'

Steven had already given up his London flat and, over the following weeks, the phone calls became less frequent and ended more quickly. The dreadful truth gradually began to dawn on her. She was losing Steven. Sarah begged him to tell her everything was all right and that they would always be together. But for the first time, he began to make excuses and tell her that perhaps it would be better if they cooled things off for a while, to allow the speculation about their friendship to blow over and for the dust to settle.

Having played a part in the breakdown of her marriage, Steven was now telling her that their affair was also over. He said he would always love her, but claimed he was not wealthy enough to marry a Duchess and support her two children. So he upped and left, leaving Sarah a broken woman with shattered dreams.

In the days that followed, I tried my best to comfort Sarah, to stem the tears that rolled down her cheeks. 'How could he have done this to you?' I asked. 'Why did he tell you he loved you?' Wiping the tears away, Sarah turned to me and said, 'I don't believe they were lies. What he told me was probably the truth because I know he loved me. But now, for some reason, he just can't honour it. I thought Steven would be here for ever.'

It was the lowest I had ever seen Sarah and I wondered how she could go on. During every phone call, she would break down and tell me that her life was ruined and she didn't have the strength to carry on, 'Why has he done this to me, Vasso? I have never loved anyone as much in all my life. I feel so empty.'

She would have done anything within her power to win back his love, but, deep down, she knew there was nothing she could do and it was tearing her apart inside. She loved Steven, the girls loved him, and he genuinely loved them, which was so important to Sarah. Steven was great with the children and although he could never replace their father — not that Sarah would have wanted him to —they had at least *seemed* like a family when they were together. He was particularly fond of Eugenie, which was hardly surprising as he had had such an intimate relationship with Sarah while she was carrying her second daughter and had spent more time with Eugenie than her own father. Sarah had been so happy that they had all got along so well. But now Steven was gone.

On a visit to Sunninghill Park shortly after the

affair ended, I found myself in the middle of a furious row between Andrew and Sarah. 'Is it over? Is it finally bloody over?' Andrew demanded. Sarah, tears of anger welling up in her eyes, yelled back that it was but what did he care? 'You're never here. What do you care what happens to me?' she said as Andrew stormed out of the room, leaving me to try and quell her rage. 'I've told him a thousand times that it's all over between me and Steven, but he doesn't want to believe me,' Sarah sobbed. 'He just keeps bringing it up again and again. There's nothing I can say or do to convince him otherwise. But what does it all matter anyway? Our relationship is dead and buried.'

On another occasion after Sarah's affair had ended, Andrew hit the roof when Steven's name was mentioned at a dinner party. A friend later revealed, 'Andrew stood up and flung his plate on to the table, china and glass went everywhere. Andrew was so angry that he looked fit to burst with rage. He stormed out of the room, swearing and shouting.' Andrew had certainly not been the best husband in the world but, nevertheless, he was a proud and honest man and Sarah's affair with Steven caused him a great deal of pain, anguish and, above all, humiliation.

The emotional scars left by Steven's abrupt departure are still evident today. Sarah says that she understands why he left her and that she is able to forgive him, but the reality is a different story. Sarah will never forget Steven and sometimes, when she is alone and feeling depressed, she wonders why it all went wrong. 'I know he loved me and everything seemed so perfect when we were together,' she told me. 'It wasn't even as if we had grown apart. I thought he would be there for me forever. I don't think I will ever find love like that again, Vasso.'

In the months that followed, Steven still called Sarah from time to time, checking that she was all right and, absurdly I thought, always taking the opportunity to tell her about his latest business dealings. 'I know it would be easier if I didn't speak to him, but I still love to hear his voice,' Sarah told me. 'I really cannot understand what went wrong. I loved him more than anything on this earth, Vasso. I still do.' She would have done anything to win back his affections but it was too late, their time had passed.

CHAPTER EIGHT
I WANT OUT

As a result of the furore over the photographs, Sarah and Andrew were summoned to a private meeting with the Queen at her Norfolk estate, Sandringham. There, for the first time, Sarah expressed her desire for a formal separation. She told me that the Queen had listened to what she had to say, but still firmly urged her to give the marriage a little more time before making an irrevocable decision, if only for the sake of the children. Sarah agreed, although her mind was already made up and she knew a little more time would not make the slightest difference. As far as she was concerned, the marriage was over. 'I made the right noises, Vasso, but it's too late for a reconciliation, far too late for that. I just want my freedom back and getting away from Andrew is the only way I'll ever be able to have it. They (the Family) don't understand or appreciate what I've been through. It's all so easy for them, they just close ranks and say nothing. They pretend that nothing's wrong. That's their way of doing things. But they've got each other, they're all family. I'm out on a limb with no one to support me or back me up.'

During those troubled days, I spent many hours discussing the situation with Sarah who explained that she simply couldn't go on living a lie. 'I've made up my mind, I want out,' she told me, adding that Andrew had reluctantly agreed to a separation and they had had several long and civil discussions about their futures, even down to the nitty-gritty of who would get what, where they would live and, most importantly, ensuring that their daughters were distressed as little as possible.

Sarah told me that she had been a bag of nerves after being summoned to Buckingham Palace for a further meeting with the Queen, who made a final, vain plea to try to save the marriage. 'Meeting my mother-in-law was the most nerve-wracking moment of all because of what I had to tell her,' Sarah told me. She said the Queen had been heartbroken at her decision, but realistic enough to see a separation was probably the only sensible solution. Like Andrew and Sarah, her overriding priority was the children, whom she adored. The Queen had already witnessed the breakdown of her daughter Anne's marriage to Captain Mark Phillips and had been aware of the enormous public interest surrounding their children. She told Sarah that her grandchildren's well-being must come above everything else and they should be shielded as much as possible. Sarah knew it was a warning not to step out of line.

There was considerable speculation about who would stay at Sunninghill Park, but Sarah made it plain that Andrew was welcome to it. 'Andrew will stay at Sunninghill and I'll find a house to rent nearby so that he can still have easy access to the girls,' Sarah told me. 'I cannot go on living under this roof any longer. It's driving me insane.'

Belatedly realising that he was about to lose his wife for good, Andrew's attitude began to change. He knew Sarah was still adamant about a separation but, sometimes, during my visits to Sunninghill, he would raise the subject in front of Sarah, asking me to try to make her see sense and call the whole thing off. Andrew would ask why she couldn't give it just a little more time and say that he still believed they could work out their differences and make a go of their marriage.

At other times, he would wait until Sarah had popped out of the room before asking me to do whatever I could to make Sarah change her mind and stay. 'I know some of the problems are of my own making, but I honestly think we can make a go of it if only Sarah would give me the chance,' he would say.

'Please tell her to stay, Vasso. I love her very much. I've tried talking to her but she won't listen to me. Will you try to make her see sense?' Andrew struck me as being very warm and genuine and I told him that I would do what I could. But I warned him his wife was a very headstrong woman who did what she wanted to do and I rather felt he had left it all too late. 'Why did you leave it all this time before realising what a good wife you have in Sarah?' I asked him. He could only shrug his shoulders. I kept my word and tried to talk to Sarah, but her mind was made up and for her there would be no turning back.

Andrew was very angry with Diana, believing she had done nothing to prevent Sarah from leaving him: 'That woman is pathetic,' he once told Sarah in front of me after the Queen had asked to see Diana at Buckingham Palace. 'She loves feeling involved in other people's problems because her own life is in such a mess. No one at the Palace has got any time for her any more. Everyone knows what she's like. I just wish she could keep her nose out of our affairs.'

The more I saw of Andrew, the more I grew to like him. He was not at all like his public image. Rather than being aloof and a bit of a buffoon, he came across as caring and thoughtful. Sometimes he seemed so depressed at the thought of losing his wife that I wished to God I could make Sarah change her mind. If only he hadn't been so thoughtless while he was away at sea then none of this dreadful business need ever have happened. If he had shown the same compassion then, instead of burying himself in his work, I'm sure they could have had the perfect marriage. It broke my heart that two people so ideally suited to one another could have dug themselves into such a terrible mess.

The days of heated arguments and fights between them had passed. But, deep down, I knew both were hurting inside. Andrew still hoped he could persuade her to stay, that he would suddenly wake up and the nightmare would be over, and they would once again be a loving family and live happily ever after. But he knew he was fighting a losing battle. For Sarah, the days when she would have considered a reconciliation had long gone. She believed a separation was the only way forward, the only chance she had of picking up the pieces of her life and starting again.

Steven may have walked out of her life but she knew it was a hopeless task trying to work things out with Andrew. She said in a revealing interview at the time, 'I just want to get away. To get away from the System and people saying no you can't, no you can't, no you can't. That's what the System is.'

She revealed how the pressures of Royal life had gradually worn her down until she felt she was actually 'owned' by the Royal Family, which was when she had turned to God for help. She said, 'A lot of people think that I'm very strong but when it comes to the Duke of

York, he is the Queen's second son and his decision goes. I supported that. The day I married him, I said I would obey him.' She also revealed the strain of constantly living in the public eye: 'Sunninghill will do to get away, but not really, because you're always on show. You've got to accept that. There are times when I give everyone the night off and don't have anybody in the house and then we can just be a family together. It is very difficult to get any privacy. In fact, I don't get any. If I get bad press, if I'm perceived to be a person I'm not, all I can do is keep my head down and get on with my work.'

She also spoke of her dream to 'escape' to the mountains. 'They talk to me and they're secure and I love them,' she said. 'And that's where I get my privacy and strength. But I'm not allowed to go because of being seen for various reasons ... because I'm owned. But at the end of the day you die alone ... and as long as you're kind, and you get up in the morning and you're happy to look at yourself ... and you're straightforward and thank God for everything you do ... because He knows. And they can write what they want to write.'

CHAPTER NINE
THE END OF THE MARRIAGE

From the beginning of 1992, the 'will they, won't they' stories about Andrew and Sarah's separation appeared in newspapers on an almost daily basis, fuelled by the fact that they had not been seen in public together since the traditional Royal gathering at Sandringham at Christmas.

Sarah rang almost every day, asking for a reading and telling me how she was struggling to get on with her life while her marriage was being dissected by the Press. When she visited, she would tell me how the pressure of having her life so closely scrutinised had left her feeling at an all-time low. Her nerves were frayed and she was staying at home and eating for the sake of it which, instead of cheering her up, left her feeling even more miserable because she was putting on weight. She was frightened of doing or saying anything in case it was interpreted wrongly and she felt that the best thing she could do was lock herself away from the outside world. 'That way, nobody will be able to say a thing,' she said. 'I don't know how much longer I can go on like this. It's eating away at me, leaving me feeling wretched and miserable. It's making me ill, it really is.'

Then in February, the fact that Sarah had been visiting me became public knowledge when the *Daily Mirror* printed a story about 'troubled Fergie' secretly visiting a 'strange Greek mystic called Madam Vasso'. This disclosure meant that my life was turned upside down overnight. After reporters had got hold of my number, the telephone didn't stop ringing and early the next morning, before I even had a chance to draw my curtains, a reporter knocked on my door ... followed by another, then another and another. There were at least twenty journalists and several television camera crews outside my house, every one of them begging me for an interview and desperate to know what a Duchess could possibly be doing visiting 'a funny little Greek fortune-teller'.

The previous day Sarah had spent nearly three-and-a-half hours at my home while, unbeknown to us, journalists waited outside. Photographers even managed to persuade someone living opposite to let them use an upstairs room so that they could secretly photograph Sarah as she entered the house and left clutching a large bunch of red roses that I had given her to try to cheer her up.

Sarah had been particularly depressed that day having heard reports from the USA that Steven had been pictured out on the town with another woman. She had already guessed that there was probably someone else in his life, but it still came as a painful blow to her, particularly as her own marriage was in such a shambles. She had made up her mind to leave Andrew, but now she suddenly began to wonder if she was making a huge mistake. Perhaps, she thought, life would be better with Andrew and the Royal Family, even with all its stifling restrictions, than without him and alone outside the Palace walls. She was torn between wanting to make a clean break and worrying that, by leaving Andrew, she would be left with no one and no protection.

She was so stressed that I spent the best part of an hour massaging her neck and back, trying to relieve some of the tension which had built up in tight knots. I asked if there was something else troubling her and she suddenly blurted out that the Queen had suggested she should see a doctor and say she was having a nervous breakdown because of all the turmoil she had been going through. She was terrified it was all part of a plot to try to take the children away from her and believed there were people who wanted to discredit her, to make out that she was mentally unstable and incapable of bringing up the girls.

'I would die if I was ever parted from my babies,' Sarah said as she burst into tears. 'They're everything to me, my whole life; without them life wouldn't be worth living.' Sarah asked if I thought she should see a doctor, as the Queen had suggested. 'Perhaps a doctor would be able to help in some way,' she sobbed. 'I don't know what else I can do. I can't fight them all by myself.' I responded by telling Sarah that she must pull herself together, that she must ignore what the Queen had told her about seeking medical help and, instead, she should hold her head up high and show everyone how strong she could be. 'It is you against them now,' I told her, 'And you must not let them beat you. If you give in now you will be finished,' I said.

I told Sarah that if she really needed to see a doctor, then she should make sure it was one she could trust and not one with any connections to the Royal Family. She went into the bathroom to splash cold water on her face and, before leaving, assured me that she would heed my advice to safeguard her children's future.

..................*

The media presence outside my house horrified me. I was worried about what my neighbours would make of the hordes of journalists camped on their doorstep and knocking on their doors trying to find out any snippet of information about me. I rang Sarah in a state of panic to tell her what was happening, and she immediately contacted Geoffrey Crawford at the Buckingham Palace Press Office who rang offering advice on how to deal with the reporters. I drew my curtains hoping that when I opened them again, it would all have turned out to be a terrible dream and everyone would have gone away. Sadly, it was several weeks before the last one finally lost interest and disappeared.

Weeks passed and still the media speculated on the state of Sarah and Andrew's marriage. The fact that she was visiting a Greek mystic, who used a plastic pyramid for her healing, gave the Press an excuse to have a field-day at Sarah's expense. 'FERGIE AND THE STRANGE GREEK MYSTIC', 'FERGIE GOES PYRA-MAD' and 'BY ROYAL AP-POINT-MENT' were among the cutting front-page headlines. It also signalled the end of Sarah's visits to my home as she was worried about being spotted and ridiculed in the newspapers. In future, we would have to meet only at her home, away from the prying eyes of the Press, she said.

Rumours of a royal split continued to intensify and, when journalists discovered that the Queen's solicitor Sir Matthew Farrer and a team of lawyers had spent most of Sunday, 15 March at the couple's home, the speculation reached fever pitch. Journalists, who were fully aware that Sarah's rota of official engagements had been suspended for some weeks, knew an announcement was imminent. The front pages of the papers carried large headlines: 'ANDREW AND FERGIE TO PART' and 'YORKS AGREE END TO FIVE-YEAR MARRIAGE'. Almost every report quite rightly alleged that Sarah's affair with Steven Wyatt had wrecked the royal marriage. Contacted at his home in Texas, Steven repeatedly denied any suggestion of a romance with Sarah. 'I have never had any romantic liaisons with the Duchess,' he said. 'We are still friends, but it is just a platonic friendship. The Duke and I are also good friends.' Steven said he was 'deeply upset' about reports of a separation, adding, 'I wish the Duke and Duchess of York the best of luck in these trying times.' Trying times indeed for Sarah, I thought, but as for Steven, he was well out of it thousands of miles away on the other side of the Atlantic. He had washed his hands of the affair, just in the nick of time he must have thought to himself, as Sarah's world continued to fall apart around her.

On the morning of 18 March, 1992, Sarah rang to tell me that a formal separation announcement would be made by Buckingham Palace the following day. But before people the length and breadth of the country learned the news, Sarah said she desperately needed to see me and sent a car to take me to Sunninghill Park. It was an incredibly fraught day for Andrew and Sarah and, as I arrived, I found them in the middle of a heated discussion in the lounge. Andrew asked if there was anything else he should know, if there was anything else she had kept from him. Sarah was in tears as she assured him that he knew all there was to know, so why did he keep having to drag everything up now that they had decided to separate? It was a futile discussion, so I interrupted saying, 'The best thing for both of you is to try to be friends. If you argue and become enemies, it is no good for the children, no good for anyone. You have the same responsibilities. Give each other time, that is so important.'

Andrew seemed rather embarrassed that I had witnessed the argument and quickly left the room. Sarah slumped down in a chair and threw her head back. She sighed, and told me it was as if a great weight had been lifted from her shoulders. 'I can't believe we've finally done it,' she said. 'It feels kind of strange, but I know it's for the best in the long run.' She told me everything had been decided and an announcement would be made the following day.

The long expected announcement that Sarah's marriage was over came, with ironic timing, at noon on 19 March, the sixth anniversary of her engagement to Andrew. Issued on the Queen's authority, the Buckingham Palace statement read:

> LAST WEEK, LAWYERS ACTING FOR THE
> DUCHESS OF YORK INITIATED DISCUSSIONS
> ABOUT A FORMAL SEPARATION FOR THE
> DUKE AND DUCHESS. THESE DISCUSSIONS
> ARE NOT YET COMPLETE AND NOTHING MORE
> WILL BE SAID UNTIL THEY ARE. THE QUEEN
> HOPES THE MEDIA WILL SPARE THE DUKE
> AND DUCHESS OF YORK AND THEIR
> CHILDREN ANY INTRUSION.

For Sarah, who for weeks had barely been able to raise a smile, the relief was immense. It was public confirmation of what the world already knew: her five-and-a-half-year marriage was finally over.

The day after the announcement, Sarah did her best to carry on with her normal daily routine, bravely managing a smile as she collected Beatrice from school shortly before midday and then returning home for more talks with Andrew, who was taking extended leave from a course at military college. The following morning, however, she was unable to stop herself from pouring out her heart to the other young mothers dropping off their children at Beatrice's nursery school. 'I just had to get things off my chest and talking to the other mothers did help me,' she said. 'Everyone is being so understanding. I think the other parents are trying to protect me from publicity by refusing to talk to the journalists who keep pestering them about what

I've been saying. I'm sure they'd rather be left in peace.'

Sarah laughed as she told me that the most amazing thing about all the fuss over the separation was that she and Andrew were still sharing the same bed! They were still good friends and had decided to forget their differences and share an intimate, candlelit dinner at one of their favourite local restaurants, the Waterside Inn at Bray. To them, it seemed like a natural way of clearing the air after the trauma of the past 48 hours, but fellow diners were shocked at the arrival of the Royal Couple who were supposedly in the throes of a bitter separation. They must have wondered what on earth was going on as Andrew and Sarah laughed and joked throughout their three-hour meal. One diner commented, 'There wasn't a hint of sadness or upset. They were affectionate with each other and friendly with the staff. They seemed to be in great spirits.'

An even more surprising development was to come the following evening when, instead of keeping a low profile at home as expected, Andrew and Sarah decided to attend a star-studded party at the nearby mansion of their friend Elton John. Again, they shrugged off the turmoil of the past week and partied until the early hours with guests including comedian Billy Connolly, rock star Sting, actor Kenneth Branagh and his wife Emma Thompson, and comedian Rowan Atkinson. Fellow guests commented on how they appeared more like a young couple deeply in love and revelling in each other's company than a couple who had just announced their separation.

They were so obviously happy and relaxed in each other's company that people, quite naturally, failed to understand exactly why they were splitting up. Sarah shrugged off the surprise at her nights on the town with Andrew, telling me that people could think what they wanted. She said Andrew felt exactly the same way and, as far as he was concerned, it was nobody else's business. 'We're still great friends and always will be, so why shouldn't we go out together and have a good time?' was how Sarah viewed the matter. 'Anyway, we had great fun and were able to forget about all the trials of the last week. It was one of the best nights I've had in ages.'

The following day was Eugenie's second birthday and Andrew and Sarah, both intent on showing family harmony for the sake of their daughters, threw a small party, inviting Sarah's father Major Ron and a few close friends. It was a wonderfully happy day, but that evening the fun of the past few days came to an abrupt end when Andrew had to pack his bags and return to the Army Staff College at nearby Camberley, leaving Sarah alone with the children. She rang saying she was totally exhausted but happy because the girls had a wonderful day with their mother and father. 'It's been quite exhausting, but the girls loved every minute of it,' Sarah told me. 'They love it when their mamma and pappa are together. It's when they're at their happiest.'

With the Press camped out on her doorstep, Sarah decided to slip away and headed for her father's home in the Hampshire village of Dummer, the village that had been put on the map and had been the focus of so much rejoicing six years earlier when it was revealed that a local girl had won the heart of the Queen's second son.

Everyone seemed to think it was now only a matter of time before Andrew and Sarah divorced and, in those early days, Sarah was no exception. At 33, she felt she was still young enough to start afresh, to start a new life away from the terrible confines of the Royal Family.

CHAPTER TEN
SARAH AND DIANA

Over the years, we often discussed Sarah's on-off relationship with Diana, which was a complicated affair, to say the very least. Sometimes, Sarah could be quite bitchy and seemed pleased when it was Diana and not her making the headlines for the wrong reasons. When critical stories about Diana appeared in the Press, her attitude would often be: 'That's the pressure off me for a few days.'

The pair had been friends since their teens and during the early days of Diana's romance with Prince Charles, it was to Sarah that she turned for help and advice over their regular lunches.

Sarah was older, wiser and certainly more experienced in the ways of the world. Sarah said that Diana could be painfully shy and, at the time, was rather naïve for her age — not something that could have been said of Sarah.

In the early days of their friendship, acquaintances told how the pair would spend hours on the telephone discussing the latest Royal gossip, a habit that has stuck with Sarah over the years, hence her colossal phone bills. Sarah was one of a handful of close friends who knew of Charles and Diana's developing relationship and one of the first to learn of the engagement. Later, it was to Sarah that Diana turned when she was feeling down while pregnant with Prince William. Sarah would often dash to Kensington Palace to try to lift her friend's flagging spirits, impressing royal courtiers with the way she seemed able to boost Diana's morale and give her the strength to cope with her new position and the responsibilities that threatened to overwhelm her.

Diana had also been largely responsible for playing match-maker, kindling the romance between Sarah and Andrew, with whom she had also had a close and warm relationship since her teenage years. Once, Diana even admitted to having had a teenage crush on him. Despite Andrew's reputation with women, she sensed his underlying loneliness and need for the security of a stable relationship. When he was pressured by Prince Philip into parting company with his long-time girlfriend Koo Stark, who many people believe would have made him an ideal wife, Diana saw Sarah as the perfect replacement and cleverly set about cultivating the relationship. The first spark of romance flickered during Ascot Week in June 1985.

Diana sensed that Sarah's affair with Paddy McNally was going nowhere and believed she would be better off with a man of her own age. I often wonder whether Diana, if she could have foreseen the troubles that lay in store for her, would have introduced one of her best friends into the Royal Family and to all the pressures and confines that came with it?

But when Sarah burst on to the Royal scene after her marriage to Andrew in 1986, she was like a breath of fresh air for Diana, someone with whom she could at last share the unique problems of life within the Royal goldfish bowl.

She looked on Sarah, who was bright and bubbly and liked by everyone, as a true friend and ally. She was someone who could bring back the fun and laughter so long missing from her own life. And perhaps Diana was also pleased that here was someone who could deflect the glare of the media spotlight away from herself.

Sarah, of course, knew she could never compete with Diana's cover-girl looks or the fact that she was considered by many to be the most desirable woman in the world. Diana always looked a million dollars in whatever outfit she wore while Sarah's choice of clothes, which at times was pretty awful, was often criticised in the Press. Initially, Sarah would just shrug her shoulders and say, 'If people don't like what I wear that's up to them. I'm happy and Andrew's happy, and that's all that matters.'

Sarah was immensely popular with other members of the Royal Family. Unlike Diana, whom they considered shy and at times rather pathetic, Sarah was full of life and brought an infectious laugh and get-up-and-go attitude to everything she did. The Queen and Prince Philip considered her a welcome addition to the Family and even Prince Charles is said to have wished that Diana could have been more like Sarah, something which would have grated on Diana and only made her feel hostile towards her sister-in-law.

Sarah told me that it was the pressures of constantly being in the public spotlight and of having their every move or words reported in the Press, that lay behind her stormy relationship with Diana. Both of them scoured the tabloid newspapers every morning and were fully aware of what was being said about them in the outside world. Sarah admitted to me that both she and Diana would sometimes get angry about snippets of gossip or alleged remarks made about each other. Sarah would tell me, 'You'd know something couldn't possibly be true, but it would niggle away in the back of your mind until you would start to wonder whether it just might be true. Of course it was a stupid way to carry on, but sometimes you just couldn't help it.'

I considered their relationship to be very sisterly:

although they frequently fell out, they always managed to kiss and make up. At the end of the day, Sarah and Diana were both Royal Family 'outsiders' and, for that reason, they always managed to sort out their differences. They are still the best of friends today.

As Sarah's affair with Steven developed, the two Royal wives spent many hours discussing ways of escaping their loveless marriages. They would ring each other at all times of the day and night, giggling like a couple of teenagers as they plotted ways of breaking free from the system they had both grown to hate. They even made a pact to leave their husbands at the same time, knowing it would be a devastating blow to the Royal Family. Sarah told me that while they could expect sympathy from some quarters, they knew there would be an onslaught of criticism from others, and by leaving together they could share the flak that would come their way.

Diana had been aware of her husband's affair with Camilla Parker-Bowles since the earliest days of her marriage. She told Sarah that she longed for a divorce so she could rebuild her life while still young enough to start afresh. Diana, who in the early days of their marriage had tried so hard to win the love and respect of her husband, claimed she would show Charles for what he really was — an adulterer. One day, she would tell the world that her marriage had been nothing but a sham. Charles and Diana didn't even sleep together.

They had separate suites and would spend much of their time locked away in solitude. Sarah told me that Diana had tried to come to terms with the fact that her husband was in love with another woman, a married one at that, believing there was nothing she could do because he was the heir to the throne. Sarah encouraged Diana to be more adventurous in the bedroom, believing that spicing up their sex life might dampen Charles' lust for Camilla. She encouraged Diana, who was rather shy and embarrassed of her body, to lead the way and experiment with different positions when making love. But nothing Diana did seemed to work.

So for comfort, she began looking to the men in her life who were closest to her — the personal bodyguards who shadowed her every move 24 hours a day. Her favourite was Barry Mannakee, a married sergeant with the Royal Protection Squad. Diana knew there were rumours about the closeness of their relationship and when he was killed in a motorbike crash in 1987, she truly believed he had been deliberately 'removed' by an organisation like the secret service, to avert a Royal scandal. Sarah told me that, in later years, Diana had used a clairvoyant to try to contact him and discover what had really happened. The episode left her terrified of exactly who was watching or listening and she would frequently have her rooms 'swept' for bugs. For many years after the accident, she would make secret visits to his graveside, praying and thinking of what might have been.

Diana, whose confidence was already fragile, became paranoid of all around her. She became so ill that she began to make herself sick after every meal and it soon got to the stage where she was unable to hold down any food. Doctors put her on medication that only seemed to make matters worse and she even made a number of half-hearted attempts to take her life, throwing herself down a flight of stairs and slashing her wrists, although Sarah said it was really just a pitiful cry for help. Sarah was genuinely worried about Diana's health and rushed to see her whenever she said she needed to talk.

One Christmas Sarah rang to tell me she was with Diana, who had been crying, and asked if I would do a reading for her. 'You wouldn't believe what she is being put through,' she said. 'You've got to help her, Vasso. We've all got to help her.' I could hear Diana whispering, asking Sarah questions that she repeated to me as I dealt out the cards. Diana wanted to know if she would ever be free of Charles but, more importantly, if she would always have custody of William and Harry if they were to divorce. What I could see in the cards worried me, for I saw a great deal of hurt and anguish. I told Sarah she must tell her friend to be positive and not to give in to the people around her. 'It is a long way off, but I see happiness and a new man who will make her feel loved and wanted again,' I said. I was certain that Diana would always have custody of the boys, but warned, 'The difficult years are not yet over. She must be strong and stand up for herself. Tell her things are not going to be easy but one day she will be free of Charles and her life will be her own again. She must have faith and believe in herself and things will work out for the best. Of that I am sure.'

Sarah said that Diana was grateful for my help and that she would call me for a reading of her own later that night. When she did ring back, Sarah again expressed her concerns about her friend's state of mind, 'Sometimes I think this family is trying to drive us both insane. I'm sure we're both looked on as troublemakers when it's really not our fault. Some of *them* are trying to make our life hell but we won't roll over and die without a fight, Vasso. We just won't. I think deep down we are both too strong for that and that's why they are so frightened of us. They just don't know what we are going to do next. And that's the trump card for both of us.'

Having made a pact and spent many long hours discussing it, Sarah was the first to make her move, telling Andrew and then the Queen that she wanted a separation. She sat back and waited for Diana to follow her example, but it became clear that Diana had no intention of doing the same. Sarah felt let down by the woman she had come to rely on as her closest friend. She was particularly angered that Diana had encouraged her to leave Andrew when she obviously had no immediate plans for leaving Charles.

For Sarah, it meant that overnight she was stopped from taking part in all official Royal engagements and tours, while Diana was allowed to carry on as usual. To me, it was a typical example of the different ways their minds worked. Sarah made a bold decision and stuck by it. Diana, on the other hand, although far from well was far more calculating. She decided to sit back, say nothing and observe how the news was received, which angered Sarah. 'We were supposed to be doing this together,' Sarah complained. 'We were supposed to give each other moral support, but now I've got to go through it all by myself. I can't believe she's let me down like this. How could she do this to me, Vasso. How could she?'

The episode left Sarah furious with Diana, because she now felt even more vulnerable and isolated within the Royal household. To make matters worse, Sarah believed that Diana was in some way responsible for leaking details of her split from Andrew to the Press. The finger of suspicion had initially been pointed at Sarah when a BBC reporter warned after a briefing with the Queen's Press Secretary Charles Anson, 'The knives are out for Fergie at the Palace.' Sarah told friends over dinner at Sunninghill, 'Well, you know who did that — that woman.' That Sarah could not even bring herself to mention Diana's name indicated just how hurt she was at what she believed to be her friend's betrayal. Sarah was worried that Andrew would believe the Palace whispering campaign that blamed her for the leaks and was greatly relieved when he assured her he knew she could not be responsible. Andrew was supportive despite the precarious state of his marriage, and told her that he, too, was convinced that Diana was to blame.

For many months Sarah and Diana rarely spoke but, gradually, they patched up their differences, only for Diana to drop her 'friend' again when Sarah was being lambasted in the Press on an almost daily basis for her freeloading antics. Sarah believed that Diana had deliberately cooled their relationship, fearing her 'saintly' image would be endangered by their association. Sarah told me that Diana was determined to be seen as 'whiter than white' in the eyes of the world and if that meant dropping a long-time friend because she was getting bucket-loads of bad publicity, then so be it.

On one occasion, when Sarah had promoted an AIDS charity, Diana demanded to know what she thought she was doing 'hijacking' a cause for which she had done so much work. Sarah was dumbstruck and very hurt when Diana slammed down the phone after a torrent of abuse. She tried to call back, but when Diana refused to take her calls she sent a fax apologising for upsetting her. 'She was furious and was yelling at me as if I had committed some terrible sin,' Sarah told me. 'I tried to explain that a friend had asked me to help out and that was all I had done, but she didn't want to know. I certainly wasn't trying to muscle in on her charity work. I would never do that. Sometimes I just don't understand that woman. It's so unfair how she suddenly turns on me. I've got enough problems with the rest of them on my back.'

It was Sarah's turn to be furious when newspapers praised Diana for her kindness in contacting a couple who had lost a young child in tragic circumstances. 'She only contacted the family after I told her I had sent the parents a little note and a picture of my two girls,' Sarah stormed. 'What I find so strange is how the Press found out she had contacted the family and yet I wasn't mentioned. It certainly makes me wonder.' Sarah was convinced that Diana had instructed someone to leak the information to the Press, knowing the story would make favourable headlines.

Sarah was forever asking about Diana during our readings, but she became deeply protective of our own relationship and once, when Diana asked her to thank me for a bunch of white roses I had sent her, Sarah flew into a tantrum. 'What's the matter? Aren't I good enough for you any more?' she demanded. I asked why she was so upset. I had sent Diana a bunch of flowers, hardly a reason to send anyone into such a rage. 'I suppose it's because she's a princess and I'm only a Duchess,' said Sarah. I told her not to be so stupid and to calm down. 'Look, if you've got anything you want to say to her you can say it through me,' she said. 'You mustn't speak to her, I'm your friend. You're supposed to be helping me. She's got her own people to talk to.'

It was typical of Sarah. She wanted my attention, all of my attention and she didn't want to share it with anyone else, least of all her sister-in-law. I explained that I had sent the flowers in the hope that Diana would ring me, because I had been getting spiritual messages from her father, the late Earl Spencer. 'You must give me the message and I will pass it on,' Sarah insisted. 'Don't contact her. Anything you need to tell her you can do through me.' A few days later, I had a curious telephone call from the *Daily Mail*'s Royal correspondent, Richard Kay, saying if I had a message for Diana he could pass it on for me. I asked how he knew I had tried to contact her and he replied that 'a friend' had told him. I know who your friend is, I thought to myself as I put down the phone, for many stories had appeared about his journalistic relationship with the Princess.

Sarah tried to hide it, even from me, but for a brief time she became incredibly jealous of Diana. It grated on her that whenever there was controversy surrounding Diana's marriage, the Press and public always seemed to take her side, but when Sarah's marriage came under the spotlight, 'fun-loving Fergie' was always the one to blame. To me, the answer was simple: Diana knew how to manipulate the Press. She knew how to make the most of photographic opportunities, deliberately ensuring she looked miserable and glum when the cameras were on her, especially when stories appeared in the newspapers about the fragile state of her marriage. In that way, she made sure that the public would blame Prince Charles and regard her as the victim. She could wrap the Press around her little finger. She was very calculating, unlike Sarah who often did things on the spur of the moment without really thinking them through.

It wasn't that Sarah wasn't clever enough to realise what Diana was doing, it was just that she refused to let others see how much she was hurting inside. Her attitude was always to hold her head up high and say, 'I'm going to be strong, I won't let them beat me, Vasso.'

CHAPTER ELEVEN
THE BRYAN AFFAIR

As the weeks passed after Sarah's split from Steven, it became clear to me that there was a new distraction in Sarah's life — in the form of Steven's distant cousin, the balding John Bryan, who had managed to worm his way into her household after being introduced to her circle of friends by Steven.

I disliked John from the first day I met him at Sarah and Andrew's home. He was wearing a baggy white track suit with a hole in the knee, and he seemed to be very casual both in appearance and in the way he behaved in Sarah and Andrew's company. She seemed completely taken in by John, a brash American whose father was of British descent, but I wasn't. Having lost Steven, although she was still deeply in love with him, Sarah seemed desperate for new affection and John happened to be in the right place at the right time. And he knew it. Unlike Steven, John relished being in the public spotlight and being linked to the British Royal Family. As soon as his distant cousin was off the scene, he set himself the challenge of trying to win Sarah's affections for himself. He was a very manipulative and crafty man who played on Sarah's vulnerability while at the same time ingratiating himself with Andrew, who was foolishly, and rather naïvely, taken in by his offers to help sort out their tangled finances and keep a protective eye on his wife.

Time after time, John insisted that he was a friend to both Andrew and Sarah and described himself to the Press as their 'financial adviser', a term that would mockingly be applied to him subsequently. Throughout the most traumatic period of the Duke and Duchess's lives, John played the role of the honest broker. He even claimed that it was Andrew who had called him in the first place, asking him to accompany Sarah on her trips abroad and to 'keep an eye out' for her welfare. Yet even before the marriage ended, Sarah and John were spotted dancing together at a trendy London night-club in December 1991, fuelling speculation about their friendship. Just two days before the separation announcement, they lunched together at a Knightsbridge restaurant, laughing and joking as they shared a bottle of expensive champagne.

The guise of financial adviser fooled few people and intrigued the cynical royal reporters, but I was one of only a handful who knew the true depth of their relationship. 'This man is no good for you,' I often warned Sarah after studying the cards, but she would just tell me not to worry and that John was a 'great friend' who was helping her sort out her life.

John was very wary of me and was irritated when I visited Sarah as he would be pushed on to the sidelines and told to keep out of the way for an hour or two, as if he was a naughty schoolboy. He would frequently come into the room where I was giving Sarah a reading and ask if she was going to be much longer. 'Out, out, out!' Sarah would say to him, laughing as she pointed towards the door. 'Vasso and I have very important things to discuss. I'll be with you when I'm ready. Now leave us in peace for a while.' John would skulk off but he was never very far away. I often asked Sarah what she saw in John, but I never once got a straight answer.

Sometimes Sarah, John and I would sit down to lunch together at the large polished table in the dining-room, where we would be waited on by one of the servants. The food, usually chicken or fish with fresh vegetables and small new potatoes, would be wheeled into the room on a gold trolley and served on beautiful china plates edged in blue and gold. There was always a choice of red or white wine from the cellar. The staff were extremely polite but John would often bark orders at them, treating them as if he owned the place. I'm sure he actually believed he was royalty. He could be very rude and I was amazed when, on one occasion, he jumped up while we were eating and switched on the television set to watch the lunch-time news. Sarah's rocky marriage was again making headlines and I felt rather embarrassed as John ranted on about the report and how the 'bloody journalist' had got some of his facts wrong. Sarah listened intently, but said nothing.

I could see that she had become very fond of John, but Steven still occupied her thoughts and she would always ask me about him during my readings. She wanted to know if he was happy, as that was very important to her even if they couldn't be together. She asked if I thought he was still thinking of her and, in her heart, I'm convinced she believed that there was a chance of one day picking up the pieces of their relationship. I'm sure John was aware of Sarah's feelings towards Steven and it irritated him intensely that he was still playing second fiddle to a man who was now off the scene. Sarah told me that he urged her to forget Steven because he had let her down so badly and caused her so much heartache. However, John was not thinking of Sarah when he offered the advice. He cared only about his own feelings and he was desperate to be Number One.

..................*

In the weeks after the announcement of the separation, Sarah had been searching for a home of her own. She wanted to find somewhere near Sunninghill Park so that the girls could easily see Andrew and their schooling would be disrupted as little as possible. She also wanted a home grand enough for a Duchess. 'I won't just settle for any old house. It has to be somewhere suitable for a Duchess.' It was reported that she had been offered a gatehouse within the grounds of Windsor Great Park, but had dismissed it immediately as 'too old and too small'. Princess Diana and every other member of the Royal Family lived in sumptuous palaces and there was no way that she was going to make do with 'some poky little backwater'.

Sarah had looked over many large properties in the area before she rang bright and cheerful one morning to tell me that she had found the ideal house — Romenda Lodge, a £1m, mock-Tudor mansion, complete with six bedrooms, swimming-pool and tennis court, set in an exclusive cul-de-sac on the Wentworth estate in Surrey. 'The gardens are wonderful, the girls will love them,' she enthused. 'It's in a bit of a mess at the moment and needs decorating from top to bottom but I can't wait to show you around. It will give me the freedom to start rebuilding my life away from the confines of that lot,' she said, referring to the Royal Family. The house backed on to the 15th fairway of one of Wentworth's famous golf courses — a course regularly used by Prince Andrew, now an accomplished player.

She laughed as she told me that the house, which would cost £6,000 a month to rent, was owned by an African chief. When the Press discovered that she was moving in, much was made of the fact that the popular show business entertainers Russ Abbot and Bruce Forsyth would be her neighbours. 'Perhaps I'll invite them to the house warming,' she joked after reading the morning's papers. Other neighbours on the estate included the actress Nanette Newman and the golfer Sandy Lyle.

As Sarah prepared to move in, a massive security operation was mounted to provide the round-the-clock armed police guard needed to watch over the young princesses, Beatrice, aged three, and Eugenie, just two. Sarah told me that concern had been expressed at the speed at which she wanted to move into the house 'but that's their problem, not mine,' she said. 'They've been complaining that I'm rushing into moving before the house is going to be ready, but I just told them to make sure it was ready! I'm fed up with waiting and the sooner I can get in the better.' The estate's wealthy residents must have been astounded at the apparently never-ending stream of furniture vans trundling up the lane, carrying everything from a massive mahogany dining-table to the starter-pack of food and wine supplied by the furniture company. 'It's a great honour to be asked to furnish the Duchess of York's new house,' said the company's Managing Director. 'We always make sure that there's a starter-pack of food and a bottle of wine. It's always handy to have some milk and tea-bags if nothing else, but I expect the Duchess may want something a little stronger.'

Sarah woke on the morning of 19 May having spent the first night in her new home. She had rung to tell me how stressful the move had been, but that she was so relieved to be finally there. 'It's such a strange feeling to have a new home,' she had told me. 'But I have good feelings about this place and am sure we are all going to be very happy here.'

The workmen hadn't quite finished and as soon as Sarah left on the school run with Beatrice who was dressed in her smart uniform and straw boater, teams of telephone engineers, plumbers and decorators began to put the finishing touches to the house. A small van arrived carrying huge sprays of Sarah's favourite flowers to brighten up every room of her new home. Keeping a close eye on all the comings-and-goings were newly erected closed-circuit television cameras, monitored by trained policemen and backed up by a team of armed officers patrolling the grounds. A 20-foot-high fence was erected at the bottom of the garden to keep out any prying eyes. Nothing was being left to chance.

Sarah had been at Romenda Lodge for less than a fortnight when Andrew popped in to have a good look around the new home. Sarah was thrilled that he had taken the trouble to visit and took great delight in giving him a guided tour. He drove off in his silver Jaguar after nearly an hour, leaving Sarah in a buoyant mood. 'You'll never guess who's just been to see me,' Sarah said when she rang me. 'Husband! He's just been to look around the house and I think he was pretty impressed. He thinks the girls will be happy here, which is so important to me. Knowing he approves has made me feel so much happier. It's given me a real lift. Everything seems so good today, Vasso. I think you had better give me a reading and tell me what the cards say. I can't remember the last time I felt so happy.'

It was about a month after she moved in that Sarah invited me to visit her at Romenda Lodge, sending a car to collect me from my home. During the journey the driver, a former military man who had been in the army for 22 years, told me about the security arrangements that had been made at the house to protect the two princesses. He said that all the staff had noticed how much happier and relaxed the Duchess had seemed since moving in. Initially, he had not wanted to work for the Duchess because of all the terrible stories he had read about her in the newspapers, but he had quickly discovered that she was an excellent, thoughtful and caring boss. He told me he had grown particularly fond of the Duchess, who was by far the friendliest member of the Royal Family. He said that Sarah called him by his Christian name, remembered the name of his wife and two children and seemed to take a genuine interest in his family. She had even sent his family gifts at Christmas, he told me. Dropping me at the door, he said he was sure I would have an enjoyable day and find 'the boss' in good spirits.

Sarah greeted me at the door with a kiss and took great pride in giving me a guided tour of the house and gardens. She had chosen all the fixtures, fittings and furniture herself, although much of it was rented, and asked for my opinion of the expensive décor. 'It is beautiful,' I assured her. 'Just right for you. You have done very well.' Sarah was delighted and gave me a big hug as she led me outside. 'I do hope the girls will be happy here,' she said. 'Andrew has promised to come and see them whenever he can and I can always take them over to Sunninghill as it's only a few miles away. It's a new home and a new beginning for me. It's all so very exciting.' She hoped that one day she might even be able to buy the house. 'I think it's just right for what I need,' she told me.

Having her own home also meant that Sarah could

see more of John, who had wasted no time in familiarising himself with her new house. John would often be at Romenda Lodge when I visited Sarah. If he wasn't there, there would be a stream of telephone calls from him wanting to know what she was up to, who she was with and what were her plans for the rest of the day. It was as if he wanted total control over her life and it worried me a great deal. 'Don't let this man control your life,' I advised her. 'Live your life the way you choose. Why does it worry him so much what you are doing?' But it didn't matter how much I warned Sarah that the relationship was destined for trouble, she carried on seeing him. 'I know you don't like him but he's been so helpful and kind with the move and sorting out the staff and the finances,' she told me. 'Just give him a bit of time and I'm sure he'll grow on you.' I quickly responded, 'Never! That man is bad news. You will see.'

When we chatted over the next few months, Sarah would often tell me that she loved John, but I was not convinced and neither, deep down, was she. 'He's been so good to me, so kind, and he's always there when I need him,' she said. 'I can always rely on him. He's such a great help.' But I believed that there was an ulterior motive with John. Yes, he was there, but while Sarah believed he was supporting her, I knew he was really supporting himself. There had always been a man in Sarah's life and John just seemed to pop up at the right time. She was in the throes of separating from her husband, shell-shocked at being dumped by Steven and John's was a convenient shoulder to cry on. And how he lapped it up!

Exactly what Sarah saw in John I never could work out. He certainly wasn't handsome and he had none of Steven's charm. He would greet me with a sickly smile, a mask that I could see straight through. I often had to bite my tongue to stop myself from telling him how rude it was to swear in front of ladies and it amazed me that Sarah never picked him up on it. She just seemed to accept it, but to me it showed John's total lack of class.

He remained very jealous of his cousin and resented the fact that Sarah still occasionally spoke to him on the telephone. John knew Steven had been the real love of Sarah's life and no matter how hard he tried he would never be able to replace him in her heart. He was no match for Steven and he knew it. He tried to persuade Sarah she would be better off ending all contact with Steven, but for his own good, not hers. It was as if he still felt threatened and knew that if Steven ever decided he wanted Sarah back, he could have her at the drop of a hat. 'I've stopped talking about Steven in front of John because he hates it,' Sarah told me. 'He gets very jealous and goes into a huff. He hates it. I shouldn't laugh but it's quite funny really.'

I think Sarah looked on John as a good friend who was always there when she needed him. He was someone who would always tell her the things she wanted to hear. She was deeply insecure and, now that Steven was no longer there, she needed someone new to tell her how wonderful she was.

Basically, she was the kind of woman who needed a man in her life at all times. She told me they had become lovers, but I don't believe she ever really loved him in the true sense of the word. 'Why do you sleep with this man?' I asked her. Sarah just shrugged her shoulders and said, 'Sometimes you just do these things, Vasso.'

John was certainly no match for Steven in the sexual stakes. But then, as far as Sarah was concerned, no one could compare with Steven in the bedroom. She would frequently tell me how they had made love for hours on end and how the nights never seemed long enough when they were together. She had never experienced love-making like it and told me she was always totally fulfilled. 'Making love with Steven is like nothing on this earth,' she would say, giggling as she told me how incredibly well-endowed her lover was. 'I just can't get enough of him, Vasso. He's the most passionate man I have ever known.'

There were never any similar boasts about John. Sarah told me about the first time she slept with him. She had been feeling particularly low, upset and alone when he had called round to visit her. It was a warm evening and they had sat in the garden at Romenda Lodge sharing a bottle of chilled white wine. 'John cuddled me to cheer me up and things went from there, it just sort of happened,' Sarah recalled. 'We ended up making love in the garden! But it was nothing special, it just happened. It didn't really mean anything.' She told me that John had a strong sexual appetite but making love with him was very different than with Steven. With John, it was more a case of having sex for the sake of having sex. Making love with Steven was totally different. She said it was as if they were one as they spent hours locked together in passionate embrace, making love in every position imaginable.

I was blunt with Sarah and told her I didn't like or trust John: 'He is only interested in himself and will bring you nothing but bad news.' But she didn't listen.

It wasn't that sex was particularly important to Sarah, it was just that she was a warm and loving person who felt she needed a strong man to support her. Being in a man's arms made her feel safe from the pressures of the outside world. She came from a broken family and throughout her life she had always searched for security. She was still a relatively young girl who needed to feel loved and wanted and, at that particular time, John happened to fit the bill.

John, like Sarah, had a very strong personality and

when he told her to sit down and listen to what he had to say she would obey him. She liked the fact that he told her what to do because everyone else around her was always *suggesting* she did this or that. John was very forceful and, unfortunately, she took notice of what he said and usually went along with his advice.

CHAPTER TWELVE
CAT AND MOUSE

Their relationship began to develop and, during the spring of 1992, Sarah and John played a game of cat-and-mouse with the Press as they travelled together in the Far East and Europe, sparing little or no thought to the damage their 'spend, spend, spend' jaunt was doing to her public image. They were spotted on the island of Phuket in Thailand, where a holidaymaker photographed them together and from there they were pursued by the Press, intrigued to discover the true nature of their relationship. 'WHERE IN THE WORLD IS FERGIE?' were among the newspaper headlines as journalists mockingly turned the affair into a world-wide guessing game to discover her whereabouts.

However, while Sarah was travelling the world and having a whale of a time, she was doing her already battered public image no good at all. For a start, she had taken Beatrice out of school during term time, angering parents and teachers alike. Second, it was revealed that she had been staying in some of the most expensive hotels in the world. There was public fury at Sarah's extravagance and senior Buckingham Palace aides were horrified at the damage she was doing to the monarchy. Prince Philip was spitting blood. Never one for holding back, the Duke dispatched a series of stinging letters criticising Sarah for her wanton disregard for the hard-working British public who were aghast at the vast sums of money she was spending. He told her bluntly to pull herself together and sort her life out. Sarah would not receive the letters until she returned home but, for the time being, she was on holiday with John and unconcerned about anyone else because she was doing what she wanted to do.

Many times since then she has looked back and realised how foolish she was in taking such a holiday, not least because she was living way beyond her means. At the time, she simply blocked the expense out of her mind and spent thousands upon thousands of pounds as if she hadn't a care in the world. Blocking things out of her mind was Sarah's way of dealing with problems. She knew her considerable financial problems wouldn't go away, but she pretended to herself that everything would eventually sort itself out. She was also convinced, having been reassured by John, that her

Budgie books would very soon make her a millionaire and she would be able to pay off her debts without a second's thought. She told herself those days were just around the corner and there was no point scrimping and saving until then, she may as well live life for the moment and pay later.

It was such a naïve way of thinking, not helped at all by John who seemed more than happy to go along with Sarah's viewpoint. I repeatedly warned Sarah to be wary of John's advice. Although he claimed to be an expert in financial affairs, I could see in the cards that money would eventually lead to his downfall and, if she wasn't careful, hers as well. 'Where is all this money coming from?' I would ask, genuinely concerned at the path her life was taking. But with Sarah it was always a case of 'don't worry, don't worry, John says everything is going to be fine'.

Sarah's friendship with John was becoming increasingly intense and, at the same time, she was starting to rely on him for advice on all her financial dealings. A woman who had lost all respect for the value of money and a man who convinced her she would soon be worth millions seemed to me to be a partnership destined for disaster. That they were sleeping together only added to the troubles I could see ahead.

Sarah told me she liked John for many reasons, not least because of the offhand way he dealt with quite senior Royal courtiers when fighting her corner. Critics rightly described John as the 'perfect networker', a man who took full advantage of both his business and social contacts, something I had warned Sarah about.

Money was at the root of much of Sarah's problems. She was wildly extravagant as she jetted from one place to the next, running up huge bills that she, not John, always picked up. She would stay in the most expensive hotels, in the most luxurious suites, then spend hours on the telephone to friends back home, running up colossal bills.

It seemed to me that she simply assumed there was an endless supply of money that she could delve into whenever she ran out. In the early days of her split from Andrew, it was this recklessness that earned her such a bad reputation. The newspapers picked up on her every trip, informing readers of 'Fergie's latest jaunt' and showing maps of how she was criss-crossing her way across the world. She had always taken a lot of holidays but now she seemed to be out of control. As one friend said at the time, 'Sarah is totally erratic with money. She'll put her hand up to bid thousands of pounds at charity auctions — money she hasn't got. She buys expensive gifts for friends and staff as well. It's something to do with playing the Royal Duchess, being the 'grande dame' at the centre of events. She certainly wasn't like that before she married the Queen's son.'

One minute Sarah would be in tears as she told me

about her latest financial crisis, the next she would be flying off across the world spending money as though she hadn't a care in the world. Sarah's life was one long roller-coaster of ups and downs, screaming along at breathtaking speed, often with little or no regard for those whose path it crossed.

Sarah was paranoid about trying to keep her affair with John secret and went to extraordinary lengths to try to maintain the charade of him being a 'financial adviser'. Following a number of Royal scandals, Sarah was particularly concerned about people listening in on her calls and devised the simplest of codes for discussing the men in her life with me on the telephone. Steven was Number One, Andrew Number Two, and John became Number Three. Another man she was later smitten with became Number Nine.

In the early days of Sarah's relationship with John, he would usually take a taxi from London and be dropped off outside a pub or a restaurant on the A30, about a mile or so from Romenda Lodge. He would ring Sarah on his mobile phone to let her know what time he would be there and she would send a car to pick him up. Sometimes, if the Press were known to be watching for the comings and goings at the house, John would tell the driver to pull over and he would jump into the boot for the last few hundred yards of the journey, only climbing out when the black wrought-iron, automatic gates had swung shut and the car had disappeared from sight. Armed officers from the Thames Valley Police, who were based at Romenda Lodge, grew increasingly alarmed at Sarah's secrecy over John and insisted that they be made aware whenever he was at the house. They argued that if there were reports of an intruder and John suddenly popped up unexpectedly he could easily find himself in the line of fire. It was put to Sarah in such a way that she had little option but to comply with their wishes.

Often John would stay for the whole weekend and, although there was the pretence of him having his own room, he would always sleep with Sarah in the master bedroom, where he even had his own wardrobe space to hang his clothes.

Sarah was worried about the effect John's presence would have on the young princesses who, it has to be said, were very fond of John and referred to him as 'JB.' Whenever he was there Sarah told me she did her utmost to ensure the girls didn't see them in bed together, always hurrying John out of the bedroom before the girls came running in in the morning. But on one occasion, Beatrice caught them together and told a member of staff, 'Mummy's in bed with John.' It must have been terribly confusing for a young child who still considered her mummy and daddy to be the best of friends.

Sarah also made sure John made himself scarce whenever she knew Andrew was coming to visit the girls or to collect them and take them back to Sunninghill Park. Andrew seemed to be one of the few people who didn't suspect his wife of having an affair with John, rather naïvely still looking on him as a mutual friend. Andrew's loyal staff, suspecting differently, would usually phone Romenda Lodge when he was on his way to visit to save him the pain of unexpectedly bumping into John, who would usually be quickly smuggled out or would lie low in another part of the house until Andrew had gone.

A member of Andrew's staff later revealed how on one occasion the usual early alarm system had failed: 'The staff at Romenda would smuggle Bryan out, then run round frantically trying to remove all evidence that he'd been there,' she said. 'One day, it all went horribly wrong. The Duke popped over with a present for the Duchess only to find Bryan playing in the pool with his children. Even then, I think, he behaved impeccably, although he did seem a little upset when he got back. There couldn't have been too much of a row because he went back later for tea.'

When Andrew and John did meet at Romenda Lodge, there was always a slightly awkward atmosphere. Andrew remained polite and courteous, but he was nowhere near as relaxed as he was when he and Sarah were alone. John always appeared embarrassed, making up an excuse to explain why he had 'just dropped in'. 'I don't want to intrude, I'll soon be on my way,' John would tell Andrew, who foolishly believed him. He even had the nerve to tell Andrew he was trying to convince Sarah to go back to him, which was the last thing on his mind. Andrew, ever the gentleman, thanked him for his kindness.

Gradually, John began to resent the fact that Sarah would not officially recognise him as her boyfriend. While Sarah was desperate to keep their affair a secret, John would have loved it to be known that he was sleeping with the Duchess. She was separated from her husband and he felt that his reputation would not suffer if people knew about his intimate Royal connections. Sure, it may harm the Duchess's reputation, but he could live with that. He was only ever interested in himself.

Sarah suspected that one of her staff was leaking details of her affair with John to the Press. So she set a trap to catch a girl who, she believed, had been going through her personal papers. Before going out for the day, she left two sealed but empty envelopes marked 'Strictly Private and Confidential' in a place where she knew only the girl she suspected would find them. On her return, she found that the envelopes had been moved ever so slightly and one of them had been opened and re-sealed. The girl had taken the bait and, needless to say, it was only a matter of weeks before the girl and Sarah parted company. 'Can you believe that from my own staff?' she asked me. 'I knew she was up to something and that was the proof I needed. Let's hope that's a warning to the others.'

Sarah lavished expensive gifts on John, foolishly believing she could buy happiness. She bought him a pair of gold cufflinks, an inscribed watch that cost thousands of pounds, and dozens of hand-made shirts. There were also funny gifts, including a pair of silk boxer shorts decorated with spotty dogs, in honour of Barclay and Lady, Sarah's two Dalmatians. In 1993, she flew him to Paris for his birthday and threw a secret party for him at a fashionable night-spot.

Another year, Sarah told him she was planning a surprise celebration and arranged to have a huge marquee erected in the grounds of Romenda Lodge. John arrived, wearing his dinner suit, and asked Sarah when the other guests would be arriving. 'You should have seen his face,' Sarah laughed. 'I told him there weren't any — it was all for him. He was most impressed. He couldn't believe it and said I was "one crazy woman".'

Sarah had arranged for a magnificent six-course dinner to be served as they sat opposite each other at a candle-lit table in the centre of the marquee. Members of staff, who had been told to wear their smartest uniforms, served Sarah's favourite champagne and vintage wine from her extensive cellar. 'Everything went so well, it was a wonderful evening,' she said. It ended with a night of passionate love-making and Sarah convincing herself that they were deeply in love.

This dinner for two illustrated two things: first, that she was an incurable romantic; and second, and more significantly, that she was becoming hopelessly extravagant in her pursuit of the high life. Friends estimated that the evening cost in excess of £8,000. Sarah had always been known for her excessive generosity but spending so much money, which she could ill afford, on a private party for two was taking things to the extreme. I asked how she could afford such extravagance, but Sarah just told me, 'Don't worry, Vasso! Everything will work out — it always does.' I responded, 'But what about the chips [the code word we used for money]? I thought you said they were still nowhere to be seen.' Sarah assured me that it was coming and then 'I'll never have any worries again'.

Her big-spending may have impressed John, but the general public was outraged at the way she frittered money away. People struggling to pay their mortgages and make a living were angered at her total disregard for money and it did little to enhance the reputation of the monarchy, already badly tarnished. 'The feeling was that she was out of control, both emotionally and financially, and it was starting to do real damage,' said one courtier.

Although Sarah knew of my feelings towards John, once when he fell ill, she rang me at home to ask if I would visit him and take some of the special Greek food I cooked for her. 'Oh pleeeese, Vasso,' she begged, like a small child trying to get her way. 'It means an awful lot to me. He's so unwell and I know you can make him better.'

I had no great wish to see him, but Sarah was worried about him and unable to get out of a dinner engagement, although obviously not that worried that she couldn't make time to go herself, I thought as I drove to Cheyne Place in Chelsea, in my silver BMW. I took with me chicken cooked with oregano, lemon soup, spinach pie, home-made bread and fresh green beans.

Sarah had rung to tell John I was coming and he greeted me at the door wearing a blue track suit. As I stepped out of the lift and into the flat, I could not believe the mess and the awful smell of take-away food that lingered in the air. The kitchen was filthy, cups were chipped and broken, the work tops were in need of a good clean and I asked how he could have let his home get in such a state. He didn't seem at all interested, shrugging his shoulders and simply moving a pile of dirty plates and cups out of the way for me. Ushering him into the living-room, I quickly began to clean the kitchen from top to bottom, washing everything in sight before preparing the food I had brought for him.

As I looked around the living-room I registered his appalling taste. The sofas were bright red and had seen better days and the blue-and-white striped cushion covers needed a wash. A signed photograph of Sarah stood on the large desk that dominated the room and there was a television and video in the corner. I commented on a large vase of fresh flowers and John said they were a present from his 'baby', Sarah. The nicest part of the two-bedroomed flat, which also doubled as his office, was the balcony and that was only because it overlooked the River Thames! I was far from impressed and wondered to myself what Sarah must make of this horrible, messy flat where, I knew, she had spent a lot of time. She was such a stickler for cleanliness and I was amazed she hadn't told him to clean up his act. Frankly, I couldn't wait to get out.

John just stood there, chatting and quizzing me about my relationship with Sarah. Later, finishing the food, he said, 'I've been pretty rough and needed that — you're a wonderful cook, Vasso. That's the first home-made meal I've eaten in a long time.' He then asked if I would be able to help him in the way I helped Sarah — by studying the cards. I took the cards out of my bag and after he had shuffled them and cut them in four, I told him he had a lot of troubles on his mind. He agreed that he had problems with his mother, his family and his business partner and asked if he was going to be successful with a deal he was trying to close abroad. We turned to more personal matters and he told me he loved Sarah: 'She's the only thing that really matters to me and, you know, one day I'm going to make her my wife.'

I said nothing, but took his words with a pinch of salt for I saw in the cards that it would not be long before he would be out of Sarah's life, although of course I did not tell him that. As I was about to leave after nearly two hours, John rang Sarah to thank her for persuading me to visit. John handed me the phone and Sarah said, 'Thank you for looking after him for me. He's a big baby who needs looking after. He told me the food was wonderful — you're such a saint.'

I visited John's flat on two other occasions, each time taking him food when he was apparently unwell. The flat was always in the same dreadful state and John would always ask for a reading before I left. Still, Sarah continued to be a regular visitor there, as it was the one place they could be sure of being alone and could make love without being disturbed.

Once, when I hadn't seen Sarah for several weeks and I knew she had been feeling particularly depressed, I rang John to ask if he would take her some flowers from me. I dropped off a large bouquet of white roses and lilies — Sarah's favourites — at his Chelsea flat and he promised to give them to her when he visited Romenda Lodge later that evening.

The following morning I rang to see if the flowers had pleased Sarah. 'The flowers were from *you*?' Sarah shrieked. 'John didn't say a word. Can you believe the cheek of it? I should have guessed as much, you always send me lilies. Just wait until I see him. I'll kill him!' I laughed and told Sarah that it must have slipped John's mind. 'A likely story,' she said. 'I just can't believe he would do something like that. I can't wait to hear his explanation.' We made a bit of a joke of it, but I hung up wondering what sort of a man John Bryan must be to stoop so low. I considered it the cheapest thing any man could do.

Something about John that had initially irritated but ultimately amused Sarah was the way he behaved in front of Diana. Sarah noticed a dramatic change in his manners and character whenever he met the Princess, oozing charm, never swearing and putting on a show of his best behaviour. 'I'm sure John fancies her,' Sarah confided. 'He puts on this terrible act, it's quite funny really.' She jokingly challenged John about his crush on a number of occasions but he had always rubbished it as 'absurd'. Sarah added, 'I know differently, a woman just knows these things, doesn't she, Vasso?' I told Sarah that it would be better for everyone if John Bryan disappeared back to the USA. 'Why you put up with this man I will never know,' I told her. 'He is always looking at other women and I promise you he is not to be trusted.'

The next time I saw John I brought Diana up in the conversation and asked what he thought of her. He told me she was a stunning lady and pointed out that they shared the same star sign — Cancer. I told him cancerian men and women often made very good couples, to which John smiled coyly and said, 'I guess that means we'd get on pretty well together then.'

..................*

John gradually began to realise how much I disliked him and did his best to try to shut me out of Sarah's life, claiming that I was trying to poison her mind. Sarah, trying to appease him, even pretended to him that she no longer spoke to me. I discovered this on one visit to Romenda Lodge. We were talking in the lounge when her butler came into the room to say John was on the telephone. She returned, her face red with rage and yelling furiously at the butler and her housekeeper Sally Fish, 'Who told him Vasso was here with me? You have no right to tell anyone my business. How dare you! Get out of my sight, both of you.' Sarah seemed terrified that she had been caught lying to John. She was in tears and her face was flushed with rage. 'I'm sorry, Vasso,' she cried. 'It's just that John thinks you are trying to turn me against him so it was easier for me to tell him that I had stopped seeing you. Please forgive me, my little friend.'

I told her not to be so foolish in letting this man have such a hold on her life. 'Be your own woman. You know you would be far better off back with your husband. John Bryan is nothing compared with him.' I had tried to make a joke of the whole episode, but the terror I had seen in Sarah's eyes had genuinely frightened me. I felt so sorry for her and wondered how she would ever be able to rid herself of such a dreadful man.

CHAPTER THIRTEEN
FALL FROM GRACE

The fall from public favour was hard for Sarah, whose popularity had soared even higher than Princess Diana's for a time. Her downfall was sealed when pictures of her having her toes kissed by John were published on the front pages of newspapers across the world. Diana may have been caught flirting with another man on the telephone, but being caught on film was another matter. People could see for themselves the true nature of her friendship with her 'financial adviser' and it seemed to me that this time they wouldn't be prepared to forgive and forget.

On 20 August, 1992, the *Daily Mirror* printed the photos that Sarah later described as the most humbling experience of her life.

The series of photographs showed a topless Sarah and John sharing the same cigarette as they lay beside the swimming-pool of the luxury £450,000 villa she was using as a hideaway near the French resort of St Tropez. The five-bedroomed house, Le Mas de Pignorol, was owned by Charles Smallbone, the former owner of the kitchen company that bore his name.

Before setting off, Sarah had told me, 'John says the villa is ideal. No one will even know we are there. I'm just going to get away from everything for a while. I'll be back before anyone even realises I'm gone.'

She had no idea how wrong John was — within hours of her private jet landing at a small airfield just a few miles from the resort, her cover had been blown and the pack of Royal reporters was on its way. Among the first to arrive was Daniel Angeli, a photographer known as the 'king of the *paparazzi*'.

All *paparazzi* seem sneaky to me, but Angeli proved to be sneakier than the rest when he gave the others the slip and headed off into the hills to find a vantage point from where he could see the goings-on at the rented villa. He was hoping for any picture of Sarah and John together, but even he could not have imagined the scenes he was about to witness. Through the telephoto lens, he watched in amazement — pound signs, no doubt, flashing before his eyes — as John massaged Sarah's legs and kissed her toes, while she in return rubbed sun cream on his balding head. The most damaging aspect of the scene he had witnessed, as far as Sarah was concerned, was that for some of the time

Andrew and Sarah share a joke at a charity golf tournament at
Wentworth in August 1995, fuelling speculation of a reconciliation.
'We're not getting engaged,' a smiling Andrew told photographers.
'In fact, we're already married!'

Above: Sarah and Steven Wyatt during the Duchess' trip to Houston, where she fell for the handsome Texan.

Below: Sarah and Steven riding in Morocco, just weeks after Eugenie's birth.

Sarah breaks down in tears at the Motor Neurone Disease Association's annual conference in September 1992 – her first public appearance after the publication of the infamous 'toe-sucking' pictures.

One of the rare occasions when Sarah and 'financial adviser' John Bryan have been photographed together.

Sarah puts on a brave face as she takes Eugenie to school for the first day of term after the much publicised toe-sucking photographs.

Above (left and right): Sarah and Ray Chambers, the American tycoon who helped bail her out of her massive debts, pictured outside the Manhattan hotel at which they were both staying in their own separate luxury suites.

Below: Official family portrait to mark Eugenie's birth, March 1990.

The photograph of America's most eligible bachelor, John F Kennedy Jnr, which Sarah cut out of a magazine believing he would one day be her husband…providing Princess Diana didn't get to him first!

Above left: Romenda Lodge: the mansion which became home to Sarah and her daughters after she separated from Prince Andrew.

Top right: Sarah's present home, Kingsbourne, on the exclusive Wentworth Estate in Surrey.

Below: Sarah and Andrew's marital home, Sunninghill Park, a £5 million wedding present from the Queen and Prince Philip.

The author, Vasso Kortesis, who became Sarah's spiritual adviser and closest confidante during the most traumatic period of her life.

Sarah visiting Vasso for a consultation at her North London home in March 1992.

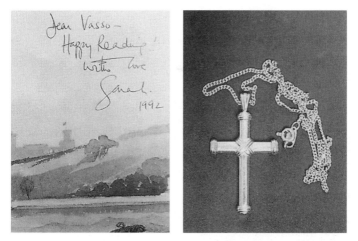

left: Sarah gave Vasso this signed copy of her book on the travels of Queen Victoria, with whom the Duchess believed she had a psychic rapport.

right: Crucifix and chain given to Vasso by Sarah as a birthday present in June 1992.

Sarah chats with Austrian tennis star Thomas Muster, known as the 'Raging Bull,' during a charity tournament in Qatar in 1995. Muster donned full Arab robes and head-dress for the occasion.

Above: Sarah's father Major Ronald Ferguson with Prince Charles at a polo match at Cowdray Park, Midhurst, in July 1987. Charles later dumped the major as his personal trainer after a series of indiscretions.

Below: Major Ron and former lover Lesley Player. Lesley went on to have an affair with Steven Wyatt.

Sarah and artist Paul Gaisford at the opening of an exhibition of his paintings at Kensington Palace state apartments. Sarah agreed to host the exhibition after falling for the gipsy artist during a family holiday with Andrew and the girls.

rah and John Bryan arrive at a small airfield on the outskirts of
Tropez for the start of their ill-fated holiday. Weeks later, the
nsational toe-sucking pictures would shock the world.

Above: Sarah's mother, Susan Barrantes, arrives to visit her in hospital for the birth of Princess Beatrice.

Below: Despite the divorce, Sarah and Andrew remain close friends and play happy families for the sake of daughters Beatrice and Eugenie at a charity golf tournament at Wentworth.

Beatrice, then just four, and Eugenie, two, were there to witness their mother's antics.

Royal correspondent James Whitaker quickly became aware of the pictures' existence and, realising their massive potential, met with Angeli and sealed a deal for his newspaper, the *Daily Mirror*, which sold an extra 1.9 million copies over the following three days.

The photographs were published. The Queen and Prince Philip were furious, the public outraged.

I had known for some time that Sarah and John were lovers but while many of the newspapers suspected it, until now there had been nothing to prove the intensity of their relationship. Now they had been caught out, the pictures finally dispelling the myth that John Bryan was simply Sarah's financial adviser. John, shown a set of prints on the night they were published, buried his head in his hands and said, 'Oh my God.' Earlier, he had been to the High Court on Sarah's behalf seeking an order to stop their publication, but the application had been rejected. He retreated to his Chelsea flat and, shortly before midnight, picked up the phone to ring Sarah who, with desperately unfortunate timing, was staying with the Queen, Andrew and other members of the Royal Family at Balmoral, the Queen's Scottish estate.

The following day, on the other side of the Atlantic, John's mother Lyda Redmond, was left worrying at the scandal engulfing her son. Speaking from her home in

Long Island, New York, she admitted that John, too, had been deeply shocked. 'The Royal Family deserve their privacy and I'm sorry if they have been upset,' she said.

At Balmoral, the publication of the photographs cast a terrible shadow over the holiday that was so important to the Queen and Sarah found herself shunned by some members of the Royal Family. For her, it was the beginning of the end. The following day, while Prince Philip and Prince Charles led guests on a shooting party, Sarah and Andrew spent many hours locked in talks, seeking a dignified way out of the crisis.

On 24 August, Sarah left Balmoral with her daughters and travelled back to Romenda Lodge, a journey seen by many at the time as the beginning of her journey into exile.

Feeling desperately low, she flew to Heathrow where a detective was waiting for her and the girls and drove them back to Romenda Lodge in a dark blue Ford Granada. Unfortunately, dozens of photographers, alerted that she had left Balmoral, were waiting and there was an almighty scramble when the electronic gates leading to her home failed to open. Sarah, agitated and trying to avoid the prying lenses, cuddled a bewildered Beatrice on her lap while the children's nanny Alison Wardley did likewise with Eugenie. A furious detective leapt out of the car, pushing the jostling photographers back and shouting 'Give her a break!' Finally, the gates opened and Sarah breathed a huge sigh of relief as the car swept up the drive to the relative privacy of her own home. Once inside, she made sure the girls were settled before telling her staff she needed a little time to herself and retired to her room. There she sat on the bed, held her head in her hands, and cried. Throughout the journey home she had been strong, strong for herself and strong for the sake of the girls. Now, alone at last, she no longer had to put on a brave face and all the anger, hurt and frustration that had been welling up inside her for the past 36 hours came flooding out. As she sat there sobbing, she asked herself again and again how *everything* could have gone so terribly wrong.

I was in Cyprus when the pictures were published and was totally unaware of the huge storm raging over their publication. It, therefore, came as quite a shock when I checked my telephone messages and discovered Sarah had rung at least a dozen times begging me to contact her as soon as I could.

I rang Sarah and realising the extent of her distress immediately booked a flight home. The following day, Sarah sent a car to collect me from my home and take me to Romenda Lodge. The area was swarming with journalists and she had told her driver to make sure I ducked down in the back seat with a blanket thrown over me to ensure I wasn't seen.

I found Sarah in a distressed and tearful state. She

said that Steven had rung her to ask if there was anything he could do to help her out of the crisis. I guessed one of the reasons he had rung was to find out the exact nature of her relationship with John, but I said nothing to Sarah as it would only have added to her woes.

The Press had been on her doorstep since the story first broke and Sarah felt like a prisoner in her own home. Outside, contractors had spent the morning increasing by another four feet the height of the fencing surrounding her home. Police were carrying out patrols, making the exclusive Wentworth estate a virtual no-go area for anyone but residents.

'What am I to do, Vasso?' Sarah asked me. She was distraught at being made to look such a fool in the eyes of the world, but the real hurt was that she had finally been caught. 'Andrew was pretty upset when he found out about the photographs,' she told me. 'He asked me how I could have been so stupid and I know he's right. God knows how I am ever going to get over this.' She told me how John had rung her with the news that the photographs had been published and how she had lain awake all night wishing the morning would never come. 'I poured myself a stiff drink, sat down in a chair and asked myself over and over again how it could possibly have happened. I went to bed but I didn't sleep. It's been like a terrible nightmare that will haunt me for the rest of my days,' she said. 'Andrew's right, how could I have been so stupid?' She was also angry with John for not finding somewhere more private for the holiday. 'He told me we'd be safe there, how the hell did the newspapers find us so easily?'

Sarah sat there crying and there was little I could do to comfort her. I had seldom seen her so low. 'This is killing me,' she cried. 'Nobody likes me any more, nobody wants me any more, everyone is pushing me away, how am I ever going to recover from this? Whatever I do goes wrong.'

I told Sarah that she could not give in now, she must pick herself up for her sake and for the sake of her children. 'Time is a great healer, my baby. Don't worry what other people are saying, worry only about yourself and your family. You must believe in yourself and have faith.'

The following week, Sarah enrolled Eugenie for a full term at her nursery, giving lie to stories circulating in the Press that she was about to quit Britain for a new life with John in the USA. She even managed a smile and a cheery wave to the photographers who had made her life a misery for the past week as she dropped Eugenie off at the Montessori school at Winkfield on the first day of term.

Wearing a smart blue skirt and jacket, Sarah spent 25 minutes talking to staff inside the tiny nursery school before being driven away by a Royal Protection Officer. School principal Bill Wilkie told reporters, 'Despite the events of the past few weeks, school is going to be as normal as ever. The Duchess chatted to me about Eugenie's lessons just like any mother would naturally do. Eugenie is enrolled for the full term otherwise we wouldn't have the security station outside so the obvious conclusion is that the Duchess plans to stay in this country. That comes as no surprise to me because she is devoted to her children and is a very good mother. As far as I can tell, the girls are her one and only priority and she cares very deeply that they should not be affected by all this.'

The next few months were particularly bad for Sarah and Andrew and their relationship hit one of its all-time lows. Andrew was hurt and humiliated by the photographs and felt everyone was sniggering behind his back, for although he had separated from Sarah, she was still his wife. She, too, was deeply wounded and blamed Andrew for the breakdown of the marriage in the first place. Had it not been for the girls, I believe it is quite possible that that would have been the last Andrew had to do with Sarah.

But the girls were there, they were the most important things in both their lives and, ultimately, it was because of them that they would begin to rebuild their damaged relationship.

Sarah's mother, Susan Barrantes, fought back publicly on her behalf, laying the blame for the marriage breakdown firmly on Andrew's shoulders.

Launching an extraordinary attack on him, she described him as 'spineless' and lacking in character. 'Andrew is a good-looking boy and has a heart of gold, to the point where he would be without any money himself to help someone,' she said. 'But he has not got any character, absolutely none. If he had, maybe his marriage would not have broken up.'

She admitted that Sarah had been saddened by what had happened in St Tropez but when asked if the Duchess was in love with John Bryan, she replied, 'I don't know. I don't want to enter into something that doesn't concern me. I only know that Sarah always knows what she is doing. She is a woman with her head screwed on. Certainly, she committed an error taking the children on holiday while she was with Mr Bryan, but you will see that Sarah will sort it out in the best way. I was the first to shout "my girl, you have really made a huge mistake. But don't worry, you must defend yourself or they will tear you to pieces".'

Angered at reports that Sarah might lose custody of her children, Mrs Barrantes added: 'My daughter is not a woman to give up easily. She knows how to defend herself tooth and nail to stop anything happening to the children. I am only sorry for Beatrice and Eugenie.'

Sarah later publicly admitted the hurt that the photographs had caused her, telling a magazine, 'I think it was the most humbling experience of my life. I will never forget it. But in retrospect I'm glad it happened. I guess it knocked everything out of me. It made me go back to look at myself and what I am all about. I was completely humiliated and the only thing I could do was turn to prayer and my faith in God and say "okay, I'm sorry, I let everybody down. Now what is the best way forward?" And so I retreated into myself and started to paint pictures. Before I wanted everybody to love me. Now I understood that I can't please everybody.'

Stories circulating at the beginning of September that a divorce settlement with Andrew would strip her of the title 'Her Royal Highness' angered and upset Sarah. The threat emerged as constitutional experts began discussing the implications of a final parting, with some suggesting she was no longer fit to hold such a distinguished title. 'Who the hell do these people think they are?' Sarah raged. 'I didn't ask for the title. I was given it and I'll bloody well keep it.' That was reinforced publicly when Mrs Barrantes told reporters Sarah had told her she would retain her title Duchess of York and would continue to be addressed as 'Your Royal Highness'.

As always, Sarah was most concerned about her daughters. 'As long as I've got the girls, I'll be alright,' she said. 'I know Andrew would never try to take them away from me and I'd never deny him access. They need both their parents around them.' She scoffed at reports that she was planning to marry John, saying,

'Vasso, why do they write these things? They haven't got a clue. I just wish they would all keep their noses out of my affairs.' Marrying John was the last thing on her mind.

..................*

At the beginning of September 1992, at Sarah's first public appearance since the publication of the photographs, she broke down in tears at the Motor Neurone Disease Association's annual conference in Birmingham.

'Everyone was being so kind and giving me so much support that I just choked,' Sarah told me the following evening. 'I was trying so hard to control my emotions but they just got the better of me. It was awful knowing everyone was looking at me as I sat there crying, but I couldn't do anything about it.' Sarah knew she hadn't really been up to a public engagement so soon after the pictures were published, but the Motor Neurone Disease Association, of which she was both President and Patron, was her favourite charity and she felt she could not let its members down. 'They were wonderful,' she said. 'People were telling me there were far worse things in the world to worry about and, do you know, Vasso, they were right. Whatever my troubles, they are nothing compared to the millions out there who have to battle against crippling disease or illness. They just pale into insignificance. I think the conference really brought that home to me. I'm fit and healthy and have two lovely daughters and I should be so grateful for that. I think I've learned a very important lesson.' I told Sarah I was very proud of her, 'No one will think any worse of you because you shed a few tears. You are only human, you have been through so much, it is only natural. You have crossed an important hurdle and you must get on with the rest of your life. Now is the time to be strong and to hold your head up high. Don't worry what others think of you, think only of yourself for once. From now on you must try not to let anyone or anything get you down. Be strong, my baby, be strong.'

Sarah's tearful breakdown led to a wave of public sympathy. It was not stage-managed and it was difficult not to feel sorry for her as she sat there sobbing with the world's Press zooming in on her reddened face. I was glad because it made people realise that, after all, she was only an ordinary young girl who had married into the Royal Family and got carried away by the status and trappings that went with it. How would anyone cope with the pressures of Royal life and the constant scrutiny that went with it, I wondered. Princess Diana was the only other woman 'outsider' to marry into the modern-day Royal Family and look how she had been unable to cope.

It was about this time that Sarah's mother rang me

from the airport after a visit to England to thank me for looking after her daughter. 'Sarah told me you gave her the strength to carry on,' Mrs Barrantes told me. 'She tells me you are like a second mother to her. I am very grateful for what you have done for her and look forward to meeting you one day.'

Sarah told me that during her visit her mother had asked for and been granted a meeting with the Queen, who she had known for many years. 'She was determined to see the Queen and to let her know her feelings,' Sarah said. 'She felt I wasn't getting the help I needed and made a personal request for the Palace to give me more support. She told me the meeting went very well.'

That December, Sarah gave an interview to an American television network describing what an awful year it had been. 'I can't go through a year like this ever again,' she revealed. 'It's too much stress ... and, of course, I brought it all on myself. I had a lot of lessons to learn and I still do make mistakes.' She spoke of Andrew as 'my best friend', adding, 'He's a lovely man who deserves to be loved.' Asked if it had been hard picking up the pieces after her separation from Andrew, Sarah replied, 'Yeah, it was hell.' Sarah said she and the princesses now spent weekends with Andrew whenever he returned from his naval duties. 'It is just straightforward family life. They love their pappa.'

When the prickly subject of John Bryan was raised,

Sarah described him as a 'fantastic friend'. Pressed with the question, 'But he was not just a financial adviser?' Sarah responded, 'I didn't say he was. He has been a fantastic friend helping me with financial work.'

Sarah was irritated when the subject of the now infamous St Tropez pictures was raised, saying, 'What is done is done and there is no good looking back over it. Let's go to the future and perhaps hope that photographers don't build trenches in woods, in seven acres of private land, two and a half miles from the road, and crawl on their tummies like snakes to get these photographs of a very happy scene, with very, very happy children. Next time I will have 15 Rottweilers wherever I go!'

Despite Sarah's comments that John was a 'great friend', the truth of the matter was that she was growing increasingly tired of him, although she dare not let on publicly for fear of offending him. She knew John could be a dangerous enemy.

I had realised for a long time that John seemed to have a frightening hold over Sarah and it worried me a great deal. But whenever I questioned her about it she just shrugged it off, saying 'Oh, he's all right.' Then she would quickly change the subject. She hated discussing John with me because she knew how much I disliked him.

Sarah decided to spend the Christmas holiday, her favourite break of the year, in Switzerland, while John stayed in the USA, skiing in Vail, Colorado. When it was suggested that, because they were apart, their relationship might finally be over, John's mother quickly stepped in to deny that was the case. 'They are very, very happy together and the children love Johnny,' she told an American newspaper. 'They didn't see each other for a few days and missed each other terribly. I don't know what will happen in the future. Sarah's children are so far from being in line for the Crown that I think divorce could be in the picture; it's much less sensitive than Diana's case. We're in the Nineties, people can be close to each other without a formal arrangement. Everything about Fergie and John is so normal. It is only because of who she is that the photos were blown out of proportion.' She went on to say that John loved Sarah's blue eyes and her skin but that 'of course, he loved her hair more than anything'.

It was a mother's natural instincts to protect her son but she, like everyone else, had no idea of Sarah's true feelings.

CHAPTER FOURTEEN
CHARITY WORK

With her private life in such a mess, Sarah threw herself into her charity work. She was determined to be seen doing good things, being positive and, at the same time, improving her public image. 'People can say what they want about my charity work but I know I'm doing it for the right reasons,' she told me. 'I know I've made mistakes in the past but I'm determined to get on with my life and do something positive. If I manage to help some people out there, I don't care what anyone else says. As long as I can keep my head down and get on with whatever I believe in, I know eventually there will be people who believe in me, too.'

People have argued, and to some extent it is true, that being seen as a 'do-gooder' was simply a way of improving her dreadful public image. Princess Diana had shown on so many occasions the PR value of cuddling a little child — it was guaranteed to make headlines. However cynically one views the matter, the truth is that it did get the charity in question benefits from the media focus on the Princess and the public awareness is stimulated.

After her highly publicised jet-setting with John, which had so angered the British people, Sarah knew she desperately had to improve her image. She was also determined to shed the 'Freebie Fergie' tag because she had been warned time and again of the damage it was doing to the Royal Family.

When Sarah launched Children in Crisis in March 1993, she did so because of her genuine wish to help underprivileged youngsters. She never went into things lightly and was determined to make it a success.

Unfortunately for Sarah, things very rarely went smoothly and the Press made much of the fact that more often than not her charity trips always seemed to involve sumptuous banquets or exotic sight-seeing excursions, which angered and upset her. 'I'm trying to help people, when are they (The Press) going to recognise that and stop attacking me?' Sarah asked me.

..................*

John was growing increasingly tired of being hounded by the Press and of his every move being watched, and

Sarah was already tired of the bad publicity every time he was involved in matters on her behalf. So, in March 1993, in a bid by him to try to escape the media spotlight and by Sarah to improve her image, John instructed his lawyers to issue a statement saying: 'Due to recent adverse publicity, John Bryan has decided to remove himself from day-to-day involvement with the media on behalf of the Duchess of York.'

The final straw for Sarah had come when a society magazine revealed the disgraceful way John had tried to negotiate a deal over a new set of fashion photographs of her, even demanding £2,500 in 'legal fees'. Sarah was forced to ring the magazine editor, apologising for the way she had been treated and saying, 'It's always me who has to carry the can. It's always me who gets the blame for this kind of thing. It's always my fault and I've had enough of it. That's why I want out of the whole thing so I can get on with my own life and stop being blamed for everything. I'm so tired of carrying the can for all of them. I've been the scapegoat of the Waleses for four years.'

The public attack on the Prince and Princess of Wales infuriated Diana who blamed Sarah for bringing her troubles on herself, mainly through her relationship with John. One of Diana's friends said at the time, 'The Princess feels it was not exactly the best thing to be photographed having your toes sucked at a French poolside by a man who was claiming to be a financial adviser. Sarah's life seems to have gone downhill since John Bryan became such an influence on her.'

Days later, Sarah rang saying she felt depressed and at the end of her tether. 'Why does everything have to go so badly wrong?' she asked. 'Why can life never be simple?' A friend revealed, 'It's John — he's a disaster for her. He doesn't understand how things are done in this country. He's so clumsy and cheap jack. It's dragging her down. But she doesn't realise, she won't listen. She feels so alone, so unprotected after the breakdown of her marriage to Andrew that she believes she needs him.'

Sarah's problem was that she had come to rely on him too much and was frightened of doing anything without first seeking his guidance. She trusted no one at the Palace to act for her and there was literally no one else she could turn to. She despised some of John's business methods yet she knew he was good at negotiating deals, something her position could never allow her to do herself.

..................*

Sarah firmly believed she had an almost psychic rapport with Queen Victoria and the more she delved into her history, while researching her two books on the monarch, the more she felt there were uncanny similarities between them. 'People call it a coincidence,' she claimed, 'but it's not.'

She even named Princess Beatrice after Queen Victoria's ninth and final child and Princess Eugenie was christened Eugenie Victoria Helena. Sarah became fascinated by everything to do with Queen Victoria and would frequently tell me she was convinced there was a spiritual link between them. Sometimes, when we were doing a reading, she would ask me if I could cast my mind back in time to see if the Queen had any messages for her. 'I know there is something there between us, I can feel it so strongly,' Sarah would say.

While researching her second book, *Travels with Queen Victoria*, Sarah often stopped to sketch a scene only to discover Victoria had been there before. She decided to include the 'duplicate' drawings alongside each other in the book to 'add a certain mystique'. She also claimed that, on impulse, she had decided to make a detour to some villages and found out Victoria had done exactly the same. 'Obviously, she wanted to show me where they had stopped,' Sarah added. 'I adore Victoria. She's got this huge strength, this great will, and, yet, this soft romantic side.' Sarah could so easily have been describing to a tee the way she saw herself.

At one stage, Sarah wrote to the Queen asking for financial backing to adapt a film from the books, but she received a polite letter saying Her Majesty was unable to help. Sarah was desperately upset as she was convinced that, with the right backing, the venture would be a commercial success. 'Why isn't she prepared to help me, Vasso?' Sarah asked. 'Someone is trying to stop me from making this film, but why?'

Through her contacts in the publishing world, she sought many other potential backers but was unable to find anyone prepared to finance the project. It was while researching her second book that Sarah became very close to John Bryan's business partner Allan Starkie, who accompanied her on her travels around Europe. She even thanked him in the Acknowledgements: 'He influenced the development of this book through his dedication to helping me, through his breadth of vision, and through his amazing capacity to carry out his work while helping me with mine.'

John had set up his Frankfurt-based company, Oceonics Deutschland, with Allan. This business had been established to build hospitals and medical centres in former Communist states. I often wondered about his motives, believing that, like John, he was simply using Sarah's contacts to get what he could for himself .

In October 1993, Allan accompanied Sarah on a charity mission to Albania, taking the wheel of the Children in Crisis minibus that was met by the Albanian President. Sarah recommended to the Albanian Health Minister that new hospitals be built and, shortly afterwards, Allan met an Albanian Government official in London to discuss the matter. It was a typical example of how John and Allan used their association with Sarah to open doors for them. It also reaffirmed my view that from the very day John met Sarah, he knew she would be invaluable to his business dealings and his bid to make himself rich.

CHAPTER FIFTEEN
IT'S FINALLY OVER

I found it quite extraordinary that just ten months after the publication of the now infamous photographs, newspapers were already hinting at a possible reconciliation between Andrew and Sarah. Rumours began circulating in the Press after the Queen appeared to be giving Sarah a second chance by inviting her back to Balmoral, the Scottish estate from which Sarah had fled in disgrace when the compromising pictures of her and John Bryan were published. Sarah was as surprised as anyone to be invited back into the Royal fold, telling me, 'I can't believe it. I thought I had seen the last of that place!'

Sarah realised that the Queen was determined not to distance herself from her granddaughters but, nevertheless, she was delighted to have received the invitation. She believed it was probably due to her keeping a low profile and staying out of trouble since the furore broke. One Balmoral worker said, 'Everyone is hoping this trip is more than just a get-together for the sake of the children.' Hopes of a reunion grew when, at the end of the summer, Andrew and Sarah were photographed together several times within the space of a few days.

At the same time as being welcomed back into the fold, she was about to experience the icy coldness of the Royal Family. Sarah's hopes of becoming a goodwill envoy to the United Nations were being blocked by scheming Palace courtiers. 'It's just another example of how they are trying to freeze me out,' she told me. 'They try to block anything I want to do.' She believed her hopes of becoming an envoy were dashed by some of the Queen's most senior aides who were worried that her overseas visits would detract attention from trips made by more senior Royals, such as Prince Charles and Princess Anne, the Princess Royal. Sarah also believed that Prince Philip had played a major role in the affair. It was more bitter humiliation for her and hurt a great deal, and it was yet more proof to her of the way the Palace machine was trying to isolate her. 'They just want me off the scene. Full stop,' she said, 'but I won't go down without a fight.'

For some time, Sarah had had a very uneasy relationship with Prince Philip and credited him with much of the blame for being ostracised from the Royal

Family. She was sure he could not have been in favour of her visit to Balmoral and must have been persuaded otherwise by the Queen.

From what Sarah told me, I realised he was not a particularly pleasant man. His attitude towards her and Diana was simple and blunt: if they wanted out of their Royal responsibilities, they should get out of the Family altogether. He didn't want to know about their problems. As far as he was concerned they should stop moaning and consider themselves privileged to be part of the Family.

Sarah blamed the Duke of Edinburgh for trying to turn other members of the Family, including the Queen, against her. Often he would send Sarah vicious letters saying exactly what he thought of her and blaming her for 'yet again' damaging the reputation of the Royal Family. The attacks were so hurtful they would often leave her in tears and she would ring me to ask what she should do about them. I would always tell her to say and do nothing as she would only make matters worse. Sarah told me that Diana received similar letters whenever she was making the headlines for the wrong reasons.

Sarah believed it was Philip who had her banned from the Royal homes, even at Christmas when the Queen so wanted all the family to be together. The Queen idolised Beatrice and Eugenie and continued to have a good relationship with Sarah, despite her husband's rantings and ravings. But Philip usually got his way and if he didn't want Sarah there, it would take heaven and earth to persuade him otherwise.

Sarah would often pretend that it didn't matter but deep down I knew the snubs caused her a great deal of pain. What really hurt was that Andrew never stuck up for her or insisted on her inclusion. Sarah told me, 'Andrew's great to me and very supportive of my charity work, but he just isn't strong enough to stand up to them. I don't think he ever will be.'

That, for Sarah, was the final straw. She had hoped, briefly, that he had changed and would stand up to his father and tell him to ease up on her. She desperately wanted Andrew to fight her corner, but she realised it was never going to happen and, as far as Sarah was concerned, a husband who was not strong enough to stand up to his father was not worth having.

..................*

Press speculation about a reconciliation had left Sarah angered and annoyed, particularly in light of the traumatic time she had been going through. 'How little these people know or understand,' she told me.

One morning, Sarah rang early to say she had asked to see the Queen at Buckingham Palace to discuss her separation from Andrew, who had arranged the meeting for her. She told me she was worried about the meeting and asked if I would go to her home to discuss some things that were on her mind. She sent a car to the home of her secretary, Jane Ambler, who lived just a few miles away from me near the Arsenal football stadium at Highbury.

Contrary to what many people have said, Sarah had always had a good relationship with the Queen. Andrew had always been her favourite child and she had been delighted at his choice of a wife. Sarah told me she found it very easy to talk to 'the mother-in-law' in plain language and she was usually very understanding. 'Basically, she's an incredibly sensible and down-to-earth woman,' Sarah told me. 'I respect and love her a great deal. It's the others who cause the problems.'

Sarah had made up her mind about what she was going to say, but wanted me to do a reading to tell her what I could see in the cards. 'I just want to be sure that I'm doing the right thing, Vasso.' I was worried because I saw in the cards that she still had a future with Andrew. 'Why don't you take a little more time? After all, what's the rush?' I asked her. 'You know he loves you and the girls very much. I'm sure one day you will be together again as a family.' But I was wasting my breath. 'Can you see anyone else in the cards?' was all Sarah wanted to know. 'It's too late with Andrew, it's all too late now.'

On the morning of the meeting with the Queen,

23 September, 1993, Sarah woke feeling nervous. She rang me very early saying she had hardly slept a wink. 'This meeting with the mother-in-law has been troubling me all night,' she said. 'I hope everything's going to be all right. I couldn't bear it if we fell out, she's always been so incredibly kind to me.'

Even as she was being driven to Buckingham Palace, she rang me on her mobile phone and we talked for most of the journey. 'I don't want to upset her. I just hope she understands that I can't go on like this for much longer,' she said. 'Do you think everything will be all right, Vasso? Tell me it will be, I'm getting myself in such a state.'

As soon as she left the Palace, Sarah again rang me: 'Basically, it went very well but I'm very relieved it's over.' The Queen had started by saying how pleased she was that she seemed to be getting on so well with Andrew and stressed how important that was for the sake of the children. She said the Queen sat and listened as she explained that, while it was true that she and Andrew were getting on much better and had ironed out many of their differences, they were both irritated and annoyed at the constant speculation concerning their marriage. The Queen asked Sarah to give it a little more time before taking matters further. Sarah told the Queen that she understood all she was saying, but she was tired of the daily Press speculation that she was heading for a reconciliation with Andrew.

'I told her that just wasn't going to happen,' said Sarah. 'I told her it was too late to salvage the marriage, that we were already too far apart. The Queen looked down and shook her head and I think then she realised that the marriage really was over. I could see she was very, very sad but I think ultimately she realised we couldn't go on the way we were.'

Sarah said that before she left, in an unusual act of warmth, the Queen had hugged her and said she really did understand what she was going through. She urged her to stay on good terms with Andrew and her final words had been to send her love to her granddaughters.

After consulting Andrew in the days that followed, the Queen decided it would be in everyone's best interests to take the unusual step of authorising Buckingham Palace to make a formal separation announcement. It read:

IN RECENT WEEKS MUCH HAS BEEN READ INTO THE OCCASIONAL PHOTOGRAPHS OF THE DUKE AND THE DUCHESS OF YORK TOGETHER ON VARIOUS OCCASIONS, LEADING TO UNJUSTIFIED SPECULATION ABOUT THEIR FUTURE. THEIR ROYAL HIGHNESSES WISH TO MAKE CLEAR THAT ANY SPECULATION ABOUT A POSSIBLE RECONCILIATION IS INAPPROPRIATE. THE DISCUSSIONS BETWEEN LAWYERS HAVE NOW BEEN COMPLETED. THEY ARE NOW FORMALLY

SEPARATED AND THEY WILL CONTINUE TO LEAD
THEIR OWN LIVES.

THEIR ROYAL HIGHNESSES REMAIN THE
CLOSEST OF FRIENDS AND IN THE INTERESTS
OF THEIR CHILDREN WILL SPEND AS MUCH
TIME AS PRACTICAL TOGETHER AS A FAMILY.
THROUGHOUT, THEIR PARAMOUNT CONCERN HAS
BEEN THE WELFARE OF THEIR CHILDREN, WHO
WILL CONTINUE TO LIVE WITH THE DUCHESS.
BOTH PARENTS, HOWEVER, WILL PARTICIPATE
FULLY WITH THEIR UPBRINGING.

Newspapers reported that, as part of the separation,
Sarah was paid £2m from the Queen's own fortune, but
with strict strings attached, including a clause that she
would never write a book about her life in the House of
Windsor.

The truth was that Sarah had accepted, without any
argument, a one-off, £2m settlement from the Queen,
£1.4m of which would be held in trust for her
grandchildren, Beatrice and Eugenie. It left Sarah
with just £600,000, which may have sounded a
fortune to most people, but in Royal terms it was a
relatively small amount considering Sarah's huge
outgoings.

There was no pay-off from Andrew. That would
only come if, and when, they decided to divorce,
although he would continue to pay the girls' £10,000-

a-year school fees. From then on, Sarah herself would have to meet all other expenses for her rented home, staff and any holidays she took. She told me at the time of the separation that she owed about £200,000 but the debt had been cleared by the Queen. 'It so annoys me when the papers say I'm now worth millions in my own right, it just isn't true,' Sarah told me. 'I've got to work for my living, harder now than I ever have before. I know I've got to knuckle down, Vasso, and I will. It just upsets me that people think I've got millions stashed away. I wish I had!'

The Press saw the announcement as signalling the end of a 15-month marital limbo, during which time they were living apart but not formally separated. It was also seen as clearing the way for divorce early the following year.

Sarah's spirits were lifted when the Queen's sister Princess Margaret rang to say she believed she was right in what she was doing and not to worry as everything would work out all right and she was talking from experience. Ten minutes later, Sarah told me, there was another call, this time from the Queen Mother, whose words of comfort and support meant a great deal to her at such a traumatic time in her life. 'It's so encouraging that they both took the trouble to ring me,' Sarah told me. 'At least it seems I've got some friends out there.'

....................*

Just weeks later in October 1993, many old wounds were re-opened when Steven married on the Saturday closest to her 34th birthday, October 15. 'Why the hell is he doing this to me?' Sarah asked, as Steven wedded American society beauty Cate Magennis in her home town of Waterford, Virginia. 'Doesn't he think he's hurt me enough already?'

She was aware that Steven had been seeing Cate for some time. Cate, like Sarah, was a Libran and she had often appeared in the cards when Sarah asked me about Steven. Time and again, I had warned Sarah about another woman in Steven's life but it was not what she had wanted to hear so she had always turned a deaf ear. It often puzzled me why Sarah so eagerly sought to know what lay ahead if she was not prepared to heed my warnings. I know she respected my word because I had so often been proved right in the past.

Although she had known it was coming, Steven's marriage was still another devastating blow to Sarah. Initially, she was angry with him, 'Steven is pretending, he's given himself a jail sentence with his wife and is damn well going to try to make it work because he's so stubborn. I don't even believe he loves her.'

I reminded her that it was Steven who had destroyed

her own marriage. 'I know, you are so right, Vasso,' said Sarah. 'I just wonder how he will cope with his own marriage and whether he still thinks about all the promises he made me.' How Sarah must have wished she could have been the bride that day.

She later told me that she had sent Steven and his new wife a belated wedding present and also her congratulations, which I found quite extraordinary. When I asked her why, she replied, 'Oh, I don't know, Vasso. Something inside just made me do it. I can't really explain it. Life goes on, doesn't it?'

Months later, she even met Steven and his wife when they visited England and, over dinner, discussed a joint charity venture in Russia. 'She seemed a very nice girl,' Sarah said of Cate. Sarah must have wondered how it was that Steven had this slim and attractive American girl on his arm instead of her. 'Those days are gone, Vasso,' she said. 'Steven is in the past. I had to move on or I would have gone mad.'

..................*

Sarah seemed to be forever searching for a new direction in life, hopelessly believing a new interest or even a new man would make everything better again. Her considerable financial and personal problems were simply shunted to the back of her mind as she suddenly threw herself into a new, ill-thought out plan to change her life. It was almost as if she was trying to escape from reality.

Towards the end of 1993, there were three new distractions in Sarah's life: southern Ireland, horse-riding and, inevitably, a handsome new man. Sarah began spending weekends in the picturesque fishing port of Kinsale, County Cork, a town known as the Irish playground for the rich and famous. Film-maker David Puttnam and actors Kevin Costner and Jeremy Irons were among those with hideaway homes in the area and Sarah believed it would make an ideal retreat for her and her daughters. 'I have strong vibes about the place,' she told me, adding that the voices inside her head, which she believed so often pointed her in the direction her life should move, were now calling her there.

Sarah told me she loved the wild, rugged coastline and enjoyed mixing with the down-to-earth locals, who she described as the most honest and natural people she had ever met. She loved the freedom, the fact that she was never hassled and that people just seemed to treat her as one of their own. Usually, Sarah would make her base just outside the town in the tiny village of Belgooley, at the stud farm owned by Robert Splaine, one of Ireland's leading international show jumpers, and his wife Eileen. As a youngster, Sarah had been quite an accomplished horsewoman and, as she began riding through the breathtakingly beautiful Cork countryside with Robert at her side, she quickly began to realise how much she had missed it. 'I haven't ridden since I was a child, but Robert is helping me get back on my feet,' she said. 'I absolutely love Ireland, the people are wonderful. They have been pleasant to me everywhere I go.'

Sarah was having regular riding lessons with Robert, and began viewing magnificent homes in the area, including an impressive Georgian mansion overlooking the harbour that was on the market for a snip at just under £500,000! Buying anything that would have been remotely suitable was way beyond Sarah's means, but it didn't stop her dreaming. As usual, she was ignoring the fact that she was already up to her eyes in debt. She loved to give the impression that as a Duchess she was fabulously wealthy and without a financial care in the world. People didn't know differently and she certainly wasn't going to tell them!

Calling herself Sally Metcalfe, Sarah began taking part in small local gymkhanas and was thrilled at winning one of the first she entered, picking up the princely sum of £5.00 and a red rosette for her troubles. The events were meant only to be a bit of fun but Sarah, who had always been fiercely competitive, took them very seriously and was terribly disappointed if she slipped up and finished down the field. 'If only I had done this,' or 'if only I'd done that, I could have won,' she would tell me. It amused me to see how upset she could get over something that seemed so unimportant to me.

Competing against farmers' sons and daughters in gymkhanas was not enough of a challenge for Sarah who almost immediately began setting her sights on far bigger events. Although she was beginning to distance herself from John Bryan, she continued to have her regular monthly meetings with him and Allan Starkie at which the three discussed a range of topics, including Sarah's charity work and her latest business ventures. After one such meeting, which Sarah called her 'fireside chats', she told me they had discussed a plan to buy a top-class show-jumper called Heather Blaze. Sarah believed that, under Robert's guidance and if she could shed a stone and get herself fighting fit, there was no reason why she couldn't compete at the very highest level. I laughed, thinking it a joke, when she told me her aim was to ride for Great Britain at the next Olympics. But Sarah wasn't laughing — she was deadly serious and seemed offended that I had made light of the matter.

Sarah was spending a lot of time with Robert, who she described as 'incredibly good-looking', and, although he was happily married and his relationship with her was never anything other than platonic, it soon became obvious to me that she had fallen for him. 'He's such a good rider, Vasso, and he's so handsome,'

Sarah told me. She was desperate to lose weight, not only to enhance her riding ambitions but also to make herself more attractive to Robert, with whom she was becoming obsessed. 'Robert thinks I have a chance of making it to the very top,' she said. 'I think he really understands me and treats my goals and ambitions seriously. He understands what makes me tick. We are a great team.' Sarah told me that she loved his company.

In late June, Sarah's riding ambitions suffered an embarrassing knock-back when she was thrown from a 16-hands grey gelding, Cool Curran Willow, while practising at Robert's stud the day before Beatrice's school sports day. The resulting bruised spine and concussion forced her to miss the parents' 30-yard dash at Upton House School. 'I took a nasty tumble and should really be at home resting,' said Sarah, who winced every time she lifted Eugenie on to her lap. 'But I didn't want to disappoint the girls. I've had the injury looked at and have been told it's not too serious. I've got a few bruises and have been told to rest for a couple of days.' Sarah had actually been knocked unconscious and had lain motionless on the ground for several seconds. The fall had left her and her ego badly bruised and in a great deal of pain. I think it also made her realise that her dreams of Olympic stardom may not be such a good idea after all. And when Buckingham Palace officials informed Sarah that she would never be able to take her daughters to live in Ireland because of the security implications, her love affair with the Emerald Isle fizzled out almost as quickly as it had begun.

CHAPTER SIXTEEN
AMERICAN DREAM

After the publication of the St Tropez photographs of Sarah and John, there was much media speculation that the two might try to start a new life in New York. Of course, Sarah knew she would never be allowed to take her daughters to live overseas, but a new life in the USA held considerable appeal for her and it was something she often mused about in her daydreams, just as she had once done at the height of her affair with Steven. She dreamt of being free again, of living her life out of the media spotlight and without the constant hounding by the Press. It was something she had often discussed with Diana who, Sarah told me, had similar dreams.

'Wouldn't it be wonderful to get away from everyone?' she would daydream. 'At least there I would have some privacy in my life.' She told me

America was so full of celebrities that, while her arrival may at first spark a wave of interest, it would soon die down and she would eventually be left in peace to mingle among the masses. It was an impossible dream, but one that kept Sarah awake for many a night as she pondered her future.

..................*

A dream among many Americans that was born out of Diana's frequent trips to New York was of a union between the British Royal Family and the closest the USA has to Royalty, the Kennedys.

John Kennedy Jr, then working in the Manhattan District Attorney's office, was rumoured in newspaper gossip columns to have sought the company of Diana. But I had other reasons to smile.

Sarah had often confided to me that she was secretly smitten by the handsome lawyer and son of the assassinated President.

Sarah fell for him when they stayed at the same hotel during one of her charity trips to America. On three occasions she left her suite and went down to the lounge bar, hoping she would bump into him but she missed him by minutes each time. She came home disappointed, but convinced that they were fated to be together. 'I want you to concentrate on a new man, someone very handsome and important,' Sarah told me. 'Something inside tells me we are going to be together. Somehow I think we were *meant* to be together.' She told me the man was John Kennedy Jr. 'The son of the former President?' I asked in disbelief. 'Yes, that's right, Vasso. Tell me what the cards have to say about him. Tell me if you can see us together in the future. Can you believe he was staying in my hotel and I didn't even get to meet him? I can't believe we were so near yet our paths didn't cross.' But she wasn't worried as she was sure it was now only a matter of time before they would become lovers.

We even gave him his own number — Sarah chose Number Nine — so that we could discuss him during our frequent coded telephone conversations. She would spend hours scouring American magazines for articles about him and drool over his picture: 'He's so handsome and muscular.' She even cut out and kept one picture of him crashing about in the sea in his swimming trunks. 'His body is just fantastic, he's in such great shape,' she said. 'Don't you think he bears more than a passing resemblance to Number One?' referring to Steven Wyatt. Personally, I didn't and considered the young Kennedy far more handsome, although I never let on. At the time, he was widely regarded as America's most eligible bachelor and had dated some of the world's most desirable and beautiful women, including singer Madonna and the blonde Hollywood actress Daryl Hannah.

None of this seemed to bother Sarah and, on another of her visits to New York, she even tried to arrange a dinner date with him, ringing his office more than a dozen times although on each occasion she was told he wasn't there. Then she would ring me, asking why he hadn't returned her calls but, of course, I had no idea. 'Perhaps you have rung too many times and frightened him off,' I told her. 'It is not good to chase after a man too hard. You must let him chase after you.' Sarah replied, 'But I so want to meet him, Vasso. I can't understand why he hasn't even called me. I'd love to meet him and see what he is really like. Perhaps the time isn't right yet. Do you think I am going to have to wait much longer?'

Often, Sarah would ask me to do a reading to see if I could see him in her cards. 'Tell me if you can see him and when we are going to be together,' she demanded. She dreamt that they had became lovers and asked me, 'Do you think my dream will come true, Vasso? Do you think we will be lovers?' On returning from a short holiday in Greece, I rang Sarah to tell her that I had seen both her and Kennedy's pictures on the front page of a Greek newspaper, though relating to different stories. 'We *are* fated to be together, I know we are,' she said. 'How I would love to meet him. Tell me, Vasso, do you think he will like me? I hope he won't want me to change too much. I'm sure everything is going to be fantastic. I'm sure we will make a great couple.'

The cards told me that he would eventually follow his late father into politics and become an instant hit. 'I think he will become President and I will be his First Lady,' Sarah told me. 'Can you imagine that, me living at the White House?' Sarah saw herself as a Jackie Onassis-style figure, hugely popular with the American people and admired across the world.

Sarah believed that the death of his mother had had a profound effect on the young Kennedy. 'He will need to look for someone who is strong enough to be like his mother. She was a very strong woman and it will be difficult for him to find a woman strong enough to take her place.' I told Sarah that she was a strong and beautiful woman, just right to fit the bill. 'Perhaps he is thinking about you right now,' I told her. Sarah laughed out loud, saying, 'If you are saying that, I think you must have been on the drink, on the Greek brandy. I should think I'm the last person on his mind right now. But one day, Vasso, one day.'

Sarah became more than a little jealous at the end of January 1995 when there was intense media speculation as to whether Kennedy would attend a glittering New York dinner, hosted by the media magnate Randolph Hearst with Diana as the star attraction. I asked if Sarah had ever discussed her feelings for the young Kennedy with Diana, but immediately wished I hadn't as she nearly snapped my head off, 'Of course I haven't. She has no idea of my feelings towards him. Nobody has. It's nobody else's business.' She was very concerned that Kennedy might fall for Diana and was incredibly relieved when he pulled out of the function at the eleventh hour. Diana, unlike Sarah, did eventually meet him, but not until shortly before Christmas 1995. They spent 30 minutes together at a New York hotel during one of Diana's frequent visits to America. Sarah was furious: 'He's mine! Why can't she just leave him alone? Everything's just a game to her. She likes to think she can twist every single man around her little finger. Well it won't work with John, I'm sure of that. She should just leave him well alone.'

..................*

19 March, 1994, the second anniversary of Sarah and Andrew's official separation had come and gone, leaving Sarah in a reflective mood.

She knew she could begin divorce proceedings at any time and was reminded of the fact by a flurry of newspaper stories claiming that divorce was now at the top of her agenda. 'It's funny how everyone seems to know what I'm doing when I haven't even decided myself,' Sarah told me. It was true she wanted to be free but she could see no benefit in pressing for a divorce. In any case, if there were to be divorce proceedings, she was not going to be the one to initiate them.

Her relationship with John had cooled considerably and she had dismissed any thoughts of one day becoming Mrs John Bryan. For the first time, John began to wonder exactly where he stood. He was still deeply involved in her financial affairs, but their personal relationship had been dealt a huge blow, mainly because of the damage Sarah realised he had done to her public image. It pleased me a great deal, as I truly believed Sarah would be far better off without him. She had suffered her worst publicity when he was on the scene and the sooner he was out of her life the better, I thought. Also, Sarah and John had had a huge row after a shopping trip during which he had embarrassed her by demanding in an exclusive London shop that she be given a discount on clothes. 'How dare he do that?' Sarah fumed. 'Can you imagine my embarrassment? I was disgusted.'

..................*

Sarah flew straight from a charity mission in Split in the former Yugoslavia, where she had been promoting her Children in Crisis charity, to New York for a series of business meetings that she hoped would secure her financial independence.

The Budgie books and spin-offs, such as toys and

clothing, were the one hope Sarah still had of making enough money to keep the wolves from the door. 'The American market is so vast, Vasso,' she told me. 'If these meetings are a success, it could be the end of all my troubles.' She asked for a reading to predict how the meetings would go and I told her the cards seemed to be saying favourable things to me. 'You are going to be a great success,' I assured her. 'You must be patient, bide your time and everything will work out for the best.' Sarah replied, 'Vasso, I've been patient, I need things to start happening *now*.'

Sarah and Diana's friendship had again become all-important and they turned to each other for support as each considered their fractured futures as virtual outcasts of the most famous family in the world. There had always been a special bond between them, although at times it had been stretched to the very limit, but now they realised that they actually needed each other to help tackle the problems they encountered. Both had experienced what it was like to be frozen out by the Royal Family, putting them in the unique position of being able to understand each other's fears and anxieties.

By the end of June 1994, they were regularly lunching together at Romenda Lodge, usually on a Saturday or Sunday. Sometimes they would hop into Diana's green Audi convertible and take Beatrice and Eugenie riding at nearby stables. Sarah told me that

Diana had started to ring her for the social chats they had so often shared in the early days of their friendship and I told her that the cards indicated that Diana would increasingly lean on her for support. 'Oh, she does that all the time now,' Sarah told me. 'She tells me that I'm the only person who really stays with her now.' They were, once again, the best of friends.

..................*

Andrew's feelings towards Sarah had grown fonder as the months passed by. The days of rows and bickering had long gone and they seemed far more relaxed and happy in each other's company. Based on what Andrew had told me and on what I learned from Sarah during those summer months of 1994, I knew he would readily welcome her back with open arms. The same, however, could not be said of Sarah. A reconciliation was certainly something she thought of and openly talked about with me. She knew it would give their daughters greater stability but in the next breath, she'd ask for my advice on the question of divorce! Her life was one of stark contradictions.

Half of her wanted to break free, to put the last wretched few years behind her and start afresh. But the other half couldn't quite let go. There was still a very deep bond with Andrew and, of course, there were her beloved girls. Whenever Sarah and Andrew were seen together, at school functions or charity events, people always commented on how well they seemed to be getting on. They were always laughing and joking, openly embracing and looking for all the world as if they were very much in love. Andrew always gave instructions that photographers should not be moved on — he was proud and happy to be pictured with his wife and, as long as the photographers kept their distance, it was fine by him.

They also regularly dined together and, at the end of September, a photograph was taken of them as they shared a candle-lit dinner in the corner of one of their favourite local restaurants, the Cottage Inn at Winkfield.

Fellow guests noticed how happy and relaxed they looked in each other's company. An American tourist sitting at an adjoining table commented, 'They certainly didn't behave like any estranged couple I know. They were smiling a lot and seemed very relaxed. I couldn't hear what they were talking about but by the tones of their voices and the occasional sounds of the Duchess's laughter, they seemed to be getting along just fine.' The American was absolutely right when he said they didn't appear like any usual estranged couple. They may once have been considered the most immature of the young married Royals but their relationship with one another had remained incredibly solid and, unlike Charles and

Diana, they were a good example of how separated parents should behave.

Sarah and Andrew really were the best of friends who enjoyed each other's company now more than ever. Both had matured a great deal and felt able to discuss their problems with one another. They talked about their children and Andrew roared with laughter as Sarah told him amusing anecdotes of the girls' mischievous antics. Fellow diners could easily have left convinced a reconciliation was on the cards. Sadly, it wasn't.

Andrew, of course, was deeply in love with his wife and would, I think, have welcomed her back. For Sarah, the situation was more complex. Maybe if it was *just* her husband she was going back to, she may have been prepared to give their marriage another chance. But she knew it would never be *just* him and that was why she felt unable to return to the Royal fold. She had a deep hatred of the courtiers surrounding Andrew and the Royal Family. She loathed the sycophants and the creeps and believed they had been responsible for wrecking her reputation. As one friend said, 'She believes they crucified her. She hates them and will never go back into their world, no matter what.'

Sarah even encouraged Andrew to go out with other women to 'have some fun'. The friend added, 'It's extraordinary, but Andrew doesn't even hold the toe-sucking pictures with John Bryan against her.

Somehow, she convinced him that it was all the fault of the Press.'

Sarah's father, Major Ron, was convinced the couple would get back together. In his autobiography *The Galloping Major* (September 1994), he wrote that they were very much back in love and if the outside world could see them together they would fail to understand how they could be apart. 'I believe Sarah does love Andrew and he would have her back tomorrow,' he wrote. 'Sarah would love to go back to Andrew and Sunninghill. But she is concerned that he isn't strong enough to stand up for her in the face of opposition from people at the Palace and possibly from other members of the family, though not the Queen.' And he said of Andrew, 'The truth is he has never fallen out of love with her. He has been very long-suffering and patient. I think, given a second chance, he'd be a much better husband.'

If only it was that easy! The Major, a bit of an old romantic who hadn't been particularly good at sorting out his own private life, let alone judging others, didn't fully appreciate the inner turmoil of his daughter.

Sarah said at the time, 'Andrew and I share a deep affection that goes far beyond all the problems of a separation. We really are best friends. Thanks to our affection and our joint efforts, and also thanks to Andrew's intelligence and sensibility and sense of responsibility as a father, our children never suffered any trauma due to our separation. Beatrice or Eugenie never saw any fights or arguments between us. When we separated I told them everything and that they would not lose their mother or father. They know their pappa is an officer and travels a great deal. They know he is always welcome at Romenda Lodge and that the big house where they lived before is also theirs. When Andrew is home from sea, he comes to see us or we go to see him, and the children see that we are really good friends. I give him a hug and he hugs me, and we all have a good time and are relaxed. There's no change in my attitude when their father is with us, and I think Beatrice and Eugenie get a lot of confidence from it. You know, I was very lucky to marry Andrew and I learned a lot from him.'

For all that, the truth of the matter was that Sarah was far from sure a reconciliation was what she really wanted. Yes, it was an option, but deep down she was still searching for true love. Although she tried to supress her feelings, she still believed that a new white knight who could sweep her away to a new happy life was just around the corner.

....................*

Sarah had a frank and close relationship with her father, but revelations about her private life in his autobiography left her bitterly angry and hurt. 'Can you believe it?' Sarah asked me, 'sold out his own daughter for money. He did it, I can't believe it but he did it. He needed the money so he sold his own daughter. I find it just monstrous.'

The Major had fallen out of favour with the Royal Family following a string of scandals, including his affair with Lesley Player which became public knowledge when she wrote a book about it. Ron had angered the Palace at the time of Andrew and Sarah's wedding by releasing to the Press details of phone calls from the Queen and then giving a series of embarrassing interviews on American television. It was in May 1988, however, that Palace fears about his indiscretion were confirmed once and for all when a Sunday newspaper revealed he had been regularly visiting a seedy massage parlour frequented by prostitutes in London's West End. He insisted that his trips to The Wigmore Club were innocent, but it was well-known as a VIP brothel and girls visited by the Major revealed in explicit detail exactly what had gone on there. The furore led to the Major losing his much-loved job at the Guards Polo Club when he was voted out as Vice-Chairman a few months later. Not long after that, Prince Charles unceremoniously dropped him as his personal polo manager after 21 years, leaving the Major angry and bitter.

CHAPTER SEVENTEEN
CHIPS WITH EVERYTHING!

Late one Sunday night, I rang Sarah who greeted me with her customary, 'Hello my little Greek friend, how are you?' She had been away for the weekend and, although she appeared cheerful at first, I quickly realised that she was depressed. 'Do you want to know how I am feeling?' she asked me. 'On a scale of one to ten ... zero. I'm shit, I'm feeling shit ... are you shit?' she said, as we both collapsed into giggles at her colourful language. 'Let me just get rid of all these bullying accountants that are here at the moment and I'll call you straight back.'

About an hour later, the telephone rang. 'Get the cards, Vasso!' Sarah said. 'I want to know what they tell you.' I asked what she wanted me to discuss with her and she replied, 'Me! I want to know what they tell you about me.'

'Someone is thinking about you,' I told Sarah as I laid out the cards on my living-room floor. 'Very good news is just around the corner, possibly to do with money. This good news also involves travel, there will be money at the end of your travels.'

'Is it about chips?' she asked excitedly. Chips or potatoes were our code-words for money. 'Yes, I'm sure it is,' I said. But before the good news, there will be a little bad news, a little anger, the cards told me. I also saw another visit, a journey overseas with Andrew and asked if she was planning a holiday with her husband. She said there was nothing planned, but they had recently discussed the possibility of taking the girls away together.

I remember the conversation well because it was the one occasion on which Sarah specifically asked me if I would talk about death and it was not something I liked to do. 'Is there any death around?' Sarah asked. 'I want to know what's happening; I want to know about death, there must be death around.' I asked her why on earth she wanted to talk about death to which she replied, referring to no one in particular, 'I wish they were all dead. The whole lot of them.'

The cards told me that Sarah felt that everyone and everything was her enemy. We talked about her own health and I asked how she had been feeling. 'Tired and finished and empty and no hope. No hope,' she repeated. 'No chips, no money! I just feel so despondent.'

She then told me that she had broken a promise to repay some money to the bank and it had been playing on her mind. 'I was supposed to repay some money but I didn't do it — I couldn't do it! The bank manager has been so good, he's laid his job on the line for me. He told his bosses "let her have a little more and I'm sure everything will be fine". I just hope for his sake that he's right.'

Sarah had always been pretty useless with money. She had a huge staff bill at Romenda Lodge, but still let what money she did have slip through her hands like water.

I told her that I could see there was someone in particular getting her down, making her upset and angry. 'Number Three,' she replied. 'There is a woman around him, I can see that very strongly,' I told her. Sarah said she believed John was having an affair, yet she still continued to see him. It was as if she was past caring and I told her she must pull herself together.

Sarah then told me that John owed her a great deal of money and that he constantly confused her about when he would repay it. Hopefully, she told me, he was on the way out of her life. She felt he was using her. At the time, he was flying to Florida and I distinctly remember Sarah telling me: 'He had better be careful in case he has an accident.' She repeated the words and it sent a shiver down by spine. It was as if she was wishing something dreadful would happen to him and I told her to put such thoughts out of her mind. She told me he had rung earlier that day complaining of being unwell. 'He's got a bad cough and a bad chest,' she said. 'All he ever thinks about is himself.' I asked if he was travelling with another woman, to which Sarah replied: 'Who knows? Who knows what he does any more?'

After more than an hour she rang off. 'I'm extraordinarily tired, so exhausted, but I must speak to you tomorrow. I'll call you,' she said.

The next day, Sarah was in the same sombre mood and when I asked how she was feeling she replied, 'Not good. I'm just not. I have so many problems, Vasso. It's all so depressing. It's just not going very well today. Everyone is using me, but I just don't give a shit any more to be honest with you. I'm so tired I couldn't care less about anything. I just want to give up quietly now.' I told her she must stay strong and continue to believe in herself: 'Don't let them beat you, you have been through too much to give in now.' She asked for a reading and I told her that marriage would again feature in her life in the coming years. She replied abruptly, 'Lack of marriage, maybe!'

Again the subject turned to money and Sarah reminded me that a year ago I had told her that her financial worries would not last much longer. 'You know what? I'm still in the same situation. The pressure on me is *beyond* belief. I feel like I've got a ten tonne truck on my head. I've got so many problems.' I told her I was sure my financial predictions were right, she would just have to allow a little more time. 'I've been working so hard to try to work things out but I don't seem to be getting anywhere,' she said.

The conversation turned to John and Sarah added, 'Number Three is not going to last much longer. He's on the way out. He's been using me too much.'

Then she added, 'To be honest, I don't give a shit about anything any more. I couldn't care less about anything. I'm so confused.' Although she was surrounded by people who were supposed to be helping her, she felt she was the one doing all the work. 'Why do I have so many dogs around me when I'm the one doing all the barking?' she said. 'All these people are meant to be working for me and I have to do it all myself. It's damned difficult and it all goes back to the same old chips.'

At our previous meeting, I had asked Sarah if Diana would speak to me as I was getting very strong messages that I needed to pass on to her. Sarah had obviously discussed the matter with Diana because she told me, 'I think I understand what your message was to Blondie. I think she does too. She said to me "I think I know what Vasso is trying to get hold of me about". Was it her father who was coming through to you? Was he trying to say to her "be careful, watch out, as something dreadful might happen?"'

I said that was exactly right. I had recently had a number of vivid dreams in which I could see the late Earl Spencer trying to get in touch with Diana to warn of great danger ahead. Prince Charles featured heavily in my dreams and Sarah told me Diana believed he was central to her father's warning. 'It's to do with Blondie's other half,' said Sarah. 'There's going to be a disaster, I mean huge, kaput! Something we shouldn't talk about, or even think about. You know what I mean?'

Sarah told me she had to take the children riding, but that we would speak again later that day. When she did call back, she was in an altogether happier mood and I realised that the reason for the dramatic change was that she had been joined at Romenda Lodge by Prince Andrew, who was a frequent visitor to the house.

Sometimes, she would take the children to Sunninghill, often staying Friday, Saturday and Sunday nights. Sarah loved him, but almost as if he was another one of her babies. 'He needs so much looking after you wouldn't believe it!' Sarah would tell me. They slept in the same bed, although they never made love. 'I just cuddle him, like he's a big baby,' Sarah told me.

Sarah was genuinely happy to see Andrew that day

and the dark cloud that had hung over her for the past two days seemed to have been lifted by his visit. 'I'm feeling a bit better,' she said.

Andrew was just leaving and Sarah was still saying goodbye to him as she greeted me on the other end of the phone line. Then she broke into a fit of giggles and yelled after Andrew, 'Come back here! What's that up your jumper?' Andrew had been rumbled trying to sneak out with one of Sarah's video cassettes but she wasn't going to let him get away with it. I could hear Andrew's deep booming laugh as he realised he had been caught: 'I was just going to borrow it for the night.' 'Oh, all right then,' Sarah responded, 'but make sure you don't lose it — I know what you're like!' As I waited, they repeated their goodbyes several times and Sarah told him that if he had nothing else planned he'd be welcome to pop over for dinner. They kissed goodbye and I laughed to myself as I thought how they reminded me of a couple of young lovers.

'Say goodbye from me,' I told Sarah, 'he's such a nice boy.' 'Yes, I know ... but not *that* nice,' she giggled. 'Surely you don't want me to go back to him,' she said, teasing Andrew who was still within earshot.

I told her I preferred him a thousand-fold to John Bryan. 'Yes, you're right, let's have Number Three put down,' she laughed. 'He's standing in my way to future happiness. Seriously, Vasso, he's just in the way now. I am trying to get him out of my life, slowly but surely.

At the moment he's still in Florida, thank goodness. Let's hope he stays there for good. Andrew's such a good boy. I get him over here whenever Number Three is coming. Deliberately, to help me. He laughs all the time. He loves it because he understands he's more important than Number Three.'

I told her how happy I was that she was getting on so well with Andrew, to which Sarah replied, 'I feel much better when he is around. It makes me feel so much more secure when he's here.' I wondered if John was getting annoyed. 'Yes, of course, but that's good,' she laughed.

I thought to myself how ironic it was that Sarah was using her husband to help get her lover out of her life, particularly after all the pain Andrew had been through because of her affair with John. Surely this type of thing didn't happen in the real world.

Although John would swear otherwise, I could see he was jealous of Andrew. John may have been sleeping with his wife, but Andrew had the respect that went with being the Queen's second son and was accorded to Royalty — something that John could never aspire to. Also, Andrew was a gentleman, the last thing in the world John could ever be described as. John even tried to stop Sarah from spending weekends at Sunninghill with Andrew and the children. She believed this was because he was terrified she might decide that life there wasn't so bad after all.

Sarah told me that John's business was in a terrible state and I warned her, as I had done on many occasions, that he was using her for her name and her contacts. Something in the cards had often told me he was using his love life to benefit himself financially, but now I could see nasty news coming his way.

After the Press had discovered his business problems, Sarah asked me, 'Why has it taken me so long to realise that he was using me all along for my contacts?' I wondered where he would live, adding, 'He is thinking what he can get out of you. Surely he is not coming to live with you?'

'No way,' said Sarah, sounding genuinely concerned, 'that's the last thing in the world I need. I couldn't have him living here. You don't really think he's going to ask me, do you? Don't worry, I won't let him get away with that,' she said. 'Make a thousand excuses, but don't let him stay, not even for one night,' I told her.

The cards told me that the death of their relationship was not far away now and Sarah said that was the best bit of news she had had in a long time. 'He's not your friend, he's your enemy,' I told her. 'Andrew does not like him either.' 'Oh yes, I know,' replied Sarah. 'He's told me so many times.'

I told Sarah to be extremely careful in her dealings with John. 'Make sure when he goes under, he doesn't take you with him,' I warned. 'He will end up with nothing, which is what he deserves. You deserve a lot better, my baby, so be very careful, believe nothing he tells you.' I said the other woman in John's life was about to see him for what he really was and she, too, would soon be leaving his life. 'Now she has realised,' Sarah said. 'He'll be left with no one.'

As we finished our chat, she told me that she was going to visit the Queen the following day, 'to see the mother-in-law' she joked. 'You know your husband is a very good man,' I said. Sarah responded: 'Oh, Vasso, I know, I know.' I added, 'Remember, whatever happens between you and Andrew, he is the father of your children and you must always stand up for him in front of the girls. You must always protect him or you risk damaging his relationship with them and I know that is the last thing you would ever want to happen. It is important that you maintain a good relationship with each other for in the long run you will both come to rely on each other as good friends.'

I, like so many others, dearly wanted to see them back together so later that afternoon I rang Andrew at his home to gauge his feelings, and perhaps, I thought, to do a little match-making. 'Vasso, lovely to hear from you,' Andrew said as he picked up the phone. 'I heard you speaking to Sarah this afternoon, I trust you are well?' I said he sounded in good spirits to which he replied, 'I am very happy. It's been a good day.' Andrew confided in me his true feelings and said he still hoped one day for a full reconciliation with his wife. 'I don't think there is basically a great deal wrong between the two of us,' he told me. 'I'm reasonably convinced that in time everything can be solved. We'll have to wait and see what goes on but I'm sure that time will tell.'

I told him that Sarah was still in love with him. 'Last night, she was feeling down, but I spoke to her this morning and she seems much better,' he replied. 'There's a long way to go and a lot of other things to be considered so don't hold your breath in the immediate term! There are so many things to be sorted first. We'll just have to wait and see.'

CHAPTER EIGHTEEN
MOVE TO KINGSBOURNE

When the owners of Romenda Lodge decided to sell the Surrey house that had been her home for the last two-and-a-half years, Sarah found herself faced with the prospect of being homeless. The newspapers were filled with hurtful stories claiming neighbours would be glad to see the back of her because of all the media attention she drew to the area, but the only thing troubling Sarah was being able to find a new home. Beatrice, now four, and Eugenie, three, were enrolled at Upton House School just five miles away in Windsor and Sarah was adamant that whatever happened, the girls' schooling should not be affected.

During a charity visit to New York, Sarah admitted publicly, 'I could move back to Sunninghill for a few months. My husband would be delighted.' She also raised a laugh when she dismissed reports that she was planning to move to America to set up home. 'I don't think those are my rumours. I think they are my sister-in-law's,' she said, referring to claims that Diana was also considering a permanent move to America.

She did reveal how much she liked their country: 'You have a great country and I find people much friendlier as I am getting a hard time in Great Britain at the moment.'

When the British Press got hold of the story that she was considering moving back in with Andrew, fuelling hope of a reconciliation, Sarah asked me, 'Why is everyone making such a great fuss? After all, he is still my husband.' She told me how warm and friendly the American people had been to her. 'The great thing about them is that they look for the positive aspects of my work,' she said. 'At home, everyone's just waiting for an excuse to have a go at me again. It doesn't matter whether it's business or charity work. If there's a tiny opportunity to have a go at me they take it.'

When Sarah launched the American arm of her charity, Chances for Children, in December 1994, with a reported £50,000 of her own money, questions were asked as to exactly why she felt the need to have her own charity in America. Some people immediately pointed out that it would give her a ready-made excuse to jet across the Atlantic to New York whenever she felt like it and frankly, it was hard not to agree with them.

Sarah had often told me that she loved the American people and the Manhattan district of New York was a place she found particularly warm and welcoming. If there was a place in America she would chose to live, it was there. I must admit to being among those who were puzzled by her motives for expanding her charity to America. She told me her British charity frequently received donations from wealthy Americans and she was keen to plough the money back into their country. I suspected one of the reasons was to raise her public profile over there and another was to give her the opportunity to promote her Budgie children's books.

During 1994, Sarah visited America on at least four occasions. Throughout her six-day visit in November 1994, she was accused of blurring the line between travel for charity, brokering her own business deals and living life as a party. Not that it particularly bothered Sarah what the Press was saying — Americans didn't sneer at her commercial activities in the same way as the majority of British people did.

Sarah's first public engagement on her return to Britain was to hand out presents at a Christmas party for local motor neurone disease sufferers. Quizzed by reporters on whether she had found somewhere to live yet, Sarah joked with one, 'Why, have you got a spare room?' On a more serious note, she told them she had to leave Romenda Lodge by 26 January but, as yet, she had been unable to find a suitable alternative home in the Windsor area. She also ruled out a reconciliation with Andrew, saying she wanted to maintain her independence. Sarah told reporters, 'I have got to be out by the end of January. I have been trying to find a house, but I haven't found one. I will be renting not buying. I can't afford to buy one. Contrary to what everyone thinks, I don't make £3 million a year from Budgie. I make very little money out of Budgie as the books have only just started selling again. I haven't got a settlement at the moment. If I get divorced, then I get a settlement. I'm looking around the Windsor area because I want to be close to my husband and the children's granny.'

Asked how the children were coping and what they thought about having to move, Sarah replied, 'We all work together as a team. The thing about children is that given security they will adapt to any situation. Children just need love and security and a parent who is there, or parents who are there, and they will work together as a team.' Sarah admitted that returning to live with Andrew was an option: 'I'm sure he would love me to, but I'm going to try to find somewhere of my own. The door is always open and I could go back if I wanted to.' Sarah said she would take a break from house-hunting to spend Christmas at Sandringham with the rest of the Royal Family.

Eventually she found a new home, Kingsbourne, a

luxurious house on the nearby Wentworth estate which she agreed to rent for an initial two years. Before she could move in, however, the property needed decorating so Sarah found herself having to ask Andrew if she and the girls could move back to Sunninghill for a few weeks. Andrew, naturally, agreed immediately. 'Of course you can come home —stay for as long as you like,' he told her.

However hard she tried, Sarah was never far away from controversy and, in December 1994, she again made headlines when she became the first Royal to publicly admit to having an AIDS test. During a three-day trip to Portugal to support a local AIDS charity, she was asked whether she had ever been tested. 'Yes, of course,' she replied. 'I underwent two tests, one before getting married and one for a life assurance application 18 months ago.'

The public admission was seized on by the British Press. Sarah asked me, 'Why do they always have to make such a mountain out of a molehill? I was being responsible and trying to promote AIDS awareness but, as usual, the whole thing has backfired. Why can't they just get off my back?' I told Sarah she must be careful with every sentence she uttered in public, as journalists would always be there to report her words. 'But why can't they focus on the positive aspects of what I say? Why do they always want to try to make a fool of me?' she added. It was something that angered and annoyed

Sarah a great deal. She was bitterly frustrated that the whole trip had turned out to be yet another public relations disaster. 'Sometimes I wonder why I bother at all,' she said. 'It would be a lot easier to lock myself away in a little box and say nothing.'

As 1994 drew to a close, Sarah was asked by a magazine what faults she might try to correct in herself in 1995. She answered, 'My extravagance and my lack of self-confidence, which sometimes makes me indecisive. I've been criticised so much over the past seven years that I have lost all my self-confidence and self-esteem.'

Sarah began the year determined to be more positive and confident of better times ahead. Unfortunately, it got off to a terrible start. Lord Charteris, one of the Queen's most trusted courtiers for more than 40 years, made sure of that in a magazine interview in the very first week of the year. In what was considered by many to be an astonishing attack on Sarah's character, he said: 'Quite simply, the Duchess of York is a vulgarian. She is vulgar, vulgar, vulgar, and that is it.' He said there would be no criticism of what he was saying from within Royal circles as it was only 'what everyone else thought'.

Sarah was deeply upset by the comments and was convinced the public would indeed believe that was exactly what other members of the Royal Family thought of her. The fact that it hurt so much was probably because, deep down, Sarah knew Lord Charteris' remarks echoed what Prince Philip and other members of the Family, including the Princess Royal, had been saying about her for years.

Princess Anne had let Sarah know exactly what she thought of her during a family dinner party some years earlier at which she had openly sneered at her for being an 'outsider' who had 'not the slightest idea' of what being a Royal was about. Andrew was furious at his sister's outburst and demanded an immediate apology which Sarah, who left the table in tears, later received. But the damage had been done, Sarah realising exactly what her sister-in-law really thought of her and from that day the two women barely spoke.

Despite recognising her position as a Royal outcast, Sarah remained incredibly loyal to Andrew and was angered by a newspaper report the following week, quoting her one-time friend Theo Ellert claiming Sarah had told her that sex with John Bryan had been wonderful, while Andrew had been a complete flop in bed. 'That's complete bollocks. I would never say that about Andrew,' she fumed. 'I can't understand why people say these things when they know they aren't true. I would never say anything to harm him.' Theo, a co-founder of Sarah's charity Children in Crisis, had been a frequent visitor to Romenda Lodge but Sarah assured me she had never discussed such intimate details of her personal life with her. Sarah had, however, told me that Andrew was not the most adventurous lover she had ever had and I guessed there was more than grain of truth in what had been said. Sarah had never been shy in telling me she had often had to lead the way when making love with her husband. She said that despite his 'Randy Andy' nickname, he was an inexperienced lover and she had taught him many new positions and techniques for making love. 'Andrew would say "what are you doing, no, no we can't do that!"' Sarah laughed. 'He was a bit of a prude, but he didn't complain for long. He soon got the hang of things!'

..................*

It was almost a month before the team of builders and engineers, who had worked round-the-clock, managed to put the finishing touches to the alterations and security arrangements at Kingsbourne, which police had insisted on before allowing Sarah to move into the £1m mansion. Aware of the disturbance and inconvenience the work was causing neighbours, some of whom had already complained that the area was in a state of complete chaos, Sarah sent them all a letter of apology.

One resident said, 'We had a note dropped round a couple of weeks ago saying the Duchess would be moving in in February. It apologised for any inconvenience, saying there was going to be a bit of activity and warning there may be problems with sightseers. But we weren't prepared for this. The whole road looks like the blitz. You can't get up and down the road for the lorries and workmen's vans and there is terrible noise all day long. There are contractors and engineers and workmen all over the place. The place has been turned into one big building site.'

It was not the kind of start Sarah wanted. 'I didn't want all this fuss and commotion, but the police insisted on it because of the security arrangements,' Sarah told me. 'I would have preferred to have slipped in unnoticed but unfortunately it can never be like that. It's all so wearing. Now I'm just looking forward to things settling down and being left alone to get on with my life.'

A few weeks after the move, Sarah woke me at two o'clock in the morning in desperate need of a chat. 'I'm sorry to ring so late, Vasso, I just needed to talk to you so badly,' she said. 'I feel I have been stretched to the maximum that any person could possibly be stretched to. With moving house, working on my writing and doing all the charity work there never seem to be enough hours in the day. I'm totally exhausted and yet when I go to bed at night, I can't sleep because I am so worried about everything. I'm exhausted. I don't know how I manage, I really don't know.'

She told me that everything was 'perfect' in her

relationship with Andrew and the Queen and that she was again getting on very well with Diana. 'That side of things couldn't be better,' she said. 'That side of it is perfect, I've done that. Andrew and I seem to have worked out our differences and put things back on a good footing. Now all that matters is the chips. I promised the man in charge of the chips that I would do it, so I can't let him down. I have got so much to pay back to the bank and I can't go on with no chips for very much longer.'

Sarah added, 'At least now I've moved in, I feel a little more settled. I feel sad yet happy at the same time. I feel I have grown up spiritually. I think I've been allowed to grow up — so many of my problems before were down to immaturity.' I told her she should seek support from Diana, as Sarah had helped her so many times in the past. 'You have to call on friends when you feel like this,' I told her. 'I want you to be able to smile again, to be happy and to enjoy life but you cannot do this without the support of close friends.' Sarah rang off, saying, 'Thank you for listening, it really does help me.'

The next morning, Sarah sounded a little brighter and told me she was pleased at having shed a lot of the weight she had gained due to depression and having lost faith and self-respect during the earlier, most difficult months after splitting with Andrew. Her dress size, which had ballooned to a 16, was down to a 12, and she told me, 'I just did it and I feel a million times better.'

Although many people believed Sarah had a skin thicker than a rhinoceros hide, this wasn't entirely true, and newspaper headlines describing her as the 'DUCHESS OF PORK' deeply affected her. Her self-esteem had always swung with her dress size and articles describing her as frumpy and overweight left her feeling humiliated and, at times, frightened of even being seen in public. She found it extremely difficult to shed the weight she had gained while carrying Eugenie, a problem experienced by any number of mothers. All the stories highlighting the excess pounds she had been carrying did terrible damage to her self-esteem. For months, she had been unable to shift the weight which had only made her more depressed and, consequently, she had eaten more to try to cheer herself up. It had been a vicious circle that had left Sarah feeling terribly depressed.

She explained: 'I suppose what I never really understood when I married Andrew was that I was going to be a public figure. I never anticipated that people would be telling me I was overweight. I had put on the weight after Eugeine was born, my stepfather and grandmother had both died, and there was a lot of pressure on me. People were saying I looked dreadful because I had put on weight, but they never really gave me a chance to explain.'

Publicly, Sarah claimed she had been on a strict diet for almost a year and put the weight loss down to healthy eating and a strict fitness regime. She was delighted with her new dress size, but said, 'I never fast or go without, so I'm never hungry. I feel so much better for having lost all that fat. It was only when I looked at my photograph in the papers that I realised how big I had become. I was just eating for the sake of it, because I was so depressed.'

She asked me, 'Didn't I look awful, Vasso? Losing the weight has given me so much confidence.' Initially, Sarah had worked out her own sensible diet, completely cutting out bread and fatty foods and skipping desserts. 'I'm eating lots of fresh vegetables, far healthier than before,' she added. She still ate lamb, her favourite meat, but always with lots of vegetables and no potatoes.

Talking publicly about her weight, Sarah said, 'It's not true stress makes you thin and I should know. What stress does is make you eat a lot more. I was desperate. I just had to do something.' Sarah also said her three-times-a-week workouts with fitness trainer Josh Salzmann had made her feel 'so much fitter and more alive'. She said, 'It has given me more energy, made me feel more positive and has certainly been great fun.'

The reality of the situation was that, in desperation, Sarah had turned for help to doctors who had, in my opinion, all-too-readily prescribed controversial slimming pills containing appetite-suppressant drugs. I believed the diet pills were partly responsible for Sarah's increasingly eccentric behaviour. In her phone calls she often sounded vague and distant, almost as if she wasn't really there or concentrating on what she was saying. Sometimes, it was almost as if she was losing touch with reality and it worried me a great deal. Fearing they were harming her health, I urged Sarah not to take the pills and to concentrate instead on her diet, but it was wasted breath. 'They're harmless, Vasso,' she would say. 'It's so good of you to worry about me, my little friend, but really there's no need. Everything's going to be fine. Once I've lost the weight, I won't need to worry any more.'

When it later became public knowledge that Sarah had taken the pills, their use was condemned by both the British Medical Association and the Royal Pharmaceutical Society, who stressed that any benefits were outweighed by the risks involved. British doctors, fearing people might copy Sarah, warned others against taking such pills saying they caused personality changes, ruined lives and it was far too easy for their use to be abused. Sarah's spokeswoman Kate Waddington said that the Duchess was well-acquainted with the potential dangers and had completed her treatment. 'She is fully aware of that situation and does not use them any more,' she disclosed.

CHAPTER NINETEEN
BRYAN GOING UNDER

By early 1995, stories were circulating of Bryan's worsening financial situation. Sarah always told me when a new story appeared in the newspapers and I knew it worried her. She was obsessed with money but was foolish enough, in her tenth interview with the glossy *Hello!* magazine, to bemoan how tough it was being a single mum bringing up two daughters on her own. 'I have to earn my living for me and my children,' she told the reporter. 'I have decided to concentrate on my commercial activities and cut back momentarily on my trips for charity. I have to work to earn my living, to be able to provide my daughters with a pleasant upbringing.' Not surprisingly, the article was seized on by newspapers who ridiculed her for moaning about money when she was living in a mansion and jetting off all over the world on holidays beyond the dreams of most ordinary people. The interview did, however, give the public an insight into her regrets about past mistakes. 'Sometimes, when I look back, I am embarrassed by some of my behaviour in the past,' she said. 'But I have grown up, I believe. I have learned, among other things, the value of money and to relish every minute of peace and every moment of fun with my children.'

Describing her relationship with Andrew as 'very good', she added, 'Last Easter, we spent the weekend at his home, Sunninghill, and he often comes over to Kingsbourne whenever his duties permit.'

....................*

Money was at the root of many of Sarah's problems ... it went through her hands like water. Despite reports that John had funded their trip to the Far East in 1992, it's unlikely he could have afforded it even if he had wanted to pay for it. In fact, Sarah had picked up the bill for the month-long junket. She also funded the ill-fated stay in St Tropez, telling friends everything would be all right as John had assured her that the Budgie books would make her a millionaire.

In one interview she admitted, 'I am far too spontaneous, extremely extravagant and my *joie de vivre* needs to be more disciplined.' A growing number of Sarah's charity trips were turning into public relations disasters. In May 1995, Sarah flew off on an ill-fated trip to Romania. First, she was photographed cuddling a bewildered little Romanian girl, which re-opened old wounds for a heartbroken British couple who had tried to smuggle the toddler out of the country 12 months earlier. John and Bernadette Mooney spent four months in a bleak jail in Bucharest before finally being freed and allowed to return home. Mrs Mooney's mother, Eunice Chimes, was furious at Sarah's indiscretion: 'Seeing pictures again of the child they loved and lost will only hurt John and Bernadette afresh.'

Then Sarah walked a diplomatic tightrope by accepting an invitation to attend an official reception.

The day after she returned, Sarah rang asking for a reading. I asked if she had had a good trip, but Sarah responded, 'No, no, no, it was a dreadful trip! I feel so disgusting, I'm terrible, awful. Why when I try so hard with my charity work do things always have to go so badly wrong?'

Sarah told me that she had been very disturbed by what she had seen in Romania, 'It's amazing what the Communist Party did to that country. It's all big buildings. It's horrid.'

I told her that I had dreamt about her, and Sarah replied: 'Oh right, what did I do wrong this time?' I told her not to be so foolish, it was a positive dream in which I saw her working on a film in America. 'Oh good, Vasso, that's such good news. And is it with a nice man, which man?' she asked. 'And what about the chips, will there be plenty of chips?' Suddenly Sarah broke down and began to sob, 'I'm having difficult times, very, very difficult times. The bank wants the money now. I've been struggling for five years and my overdraft is now up to £2m!' She said it was about the same amount as winning the lottery jackpot.

I told Sarah I had read a magazine article in which John had openly talked about their relationship, no doubt in return for a big pay cheque. 'Wasn't it disgusting, what he did?' Sarah said. 'Can you imagine doing that? He's not going to manage to live any more, you know he can't, not with behaviour like this.'

Although by June 1995 John was well on his way out of Sarah's life, he laughed off reports of a rift with her claiming, 'To say I'm out of her life just isn't true!' He may have known that Sarah was growing tired of him and the problems he brought, but publicly he wanted it known for reasons of his own that he and Sarah were still 'an item'.

His money troubles worsened and Sarah told me he had still failed to repay the money he owed her. The following month, Sarah publicly hinted at her own money troubles when she admitted she needed the profits from the sale of an adaptation of her Budgie cartoon to America's Fox TV network. She also said Americans should not be surprised to see Royalty dabbling in Hollywood's television industry. 'I'm 35. I'm in 1995. I've got two healthy children. I am a separated woman. I'm a working woman. Royal or not I've got to get out there,' she said, adding that although some of the profits from her books went to charity, the deal with Fox would go straight into her own pockets.

A week or so later, as Britain basked in scorching summer weather, Sarah rang. I could tell from her voice that she was depressed and had been crying. 'I just can't cope, Vasso. Not with him, Number Three, he can go to jail. I couldn't give a fuck about him. It's everything else that is getting me down, my office, the chips ... I just want a life!'

She told me she still had terrible financial problems and there was nothing she could do to ease them. Money from the sale of her Budgie books was her only hope of staying afloat, she said. 'But it just isn't coming. People keep telling me everything is going to be all right, but when? I just don't know how much longer I can go on like this.'

She talked about revelations in newspaper gossip columns that her relationship with John Bryan was finally over. 'But that is such good news,' she said. 'It's great news that they are saying Number Three and I are finished. I love that. I think he's in trouble again, big trouble, but that's his look-out!'

The papers were correct in one respect — their physical relationship had been dead for some months. I felt that John still had an incredible hold over Sarah and I came to the conclusion that, although she had made him sign a confidentiality agreement, she was terrified of him cashing in on their affair by selling intimate details of their often passionate relationship.

A few weeks later, Sarah again rang me in a distressed state: 'The pressure is getting too much for any one person to bear. Pressures from everywhere. From Number Three, pressure from the money, pressure from the bank and pressure from life.'

Sarah told me she had been speaking to Diana who believed something dreadful was about to happen to Prince Charles. 'I think he is going to have a problem, a big problem, you know? Although we shouldn't mention it, he might not go on for much longer in this life.' I asked what could possibly make her think such a thing. Sarah replied, 'Because 'D' (Diana) told me. Blondie said she thinks that. She said someone told her that and she believes it. I think she would be pleased if that happened.' Sarah told me Diana firmly believed Charles would be killed in a plane crash or a skiing accident, making Prince William heir to the throne.

Sarah returned to her own financial problems adding, 'Vasso, things are so bad financially that I just have to giggle now. The chips are nowhere to be seen. Things are getting really bad now.'

The following day Sarah rang and I asked how she was feeling: 'I'm moderate ... well, terrible actually,' she replied. 'I'm tired, so tired, I don't even get time to speak to you. It's amazing how people just aren't with you when you need them. I just hope one day I get a nice man in my life. I haven't lost my faith, Vasso, but I'm just so tired. I've got too much work to do to get the chips so I have to forfeit everything else. I haven't been talking to anybody, I've just been working to try to get some chips. The workload is phenomenal.'

I asked what had made her so depressed and she told me how hurt and upset she was at being excluded from a Royal gathering the previous weekend. 'That really hurt,' she confided.' It was dreadful. But you know they are dreadful like that. And Andrew said nothing. He didn't stand up for me while he tells me he still loves me.' I was angry with Andrew and told Sarah he should stand by her and support her. 'Why is he so kind one minute and then able to let you down so badly the next?' I asked. 'Why does he tell me he wants you back? He should put his foot down and support you. He doesn't seem to have changed at all.' Sarah replied, 'Oh, I don't know Vasso, sometimes I think he's changed and he'll stand up for me at last. Then something like this happens and I realise things are exactly as they were before. But don't worry, as soon as I get myself together I'll be fine. I just need a bit of time on my own to get my act together and then I'll be all right again. It's at times like this that I feel I have lost all my confidence and self-esteem. I wonder what everyone out there must be thinking and what they must make of me.'

Sarah asked me to concentrate on a charity visit she had been asked to make to Russia. 'I want you to think and focus and tell me what you can see about this trip,' she said. 'I don't like the feel of it, the corruption there, and I want you to tell me whether I should go or not.' The following day, I told her not to go because she would be disappointed and there would be problems with the trip. 'I know you're right, but I have just got to get out of here and away from these wretched people,' Sarah responded.

Sarah told me how she had gone to extraordinary lengths to clean up her act and shed her 'Freebie Fergie' label. 'I know I've been foolish in the past and done so many things without really thinking them through, but I have put a stop to those silly mistakes and am determined to let people see that,' she explained. 'It's just a matter of being able to combine my business and charity work, of striking the right balance.'

A friend revealed, 'Sarah feels she has to be whiter than white nowadays. She hates being seen as extravagant. Of course, when she flies she has to travel first-class because it is safer with less people gawking at her and also because it is expected of a Duchess. About one in five charity trips is 'paid for' by a sponsor, who will meet the cost of air fares and hotels, but all the other times Sarah pays her own way. She always takes someone with her because, as she is no longer entitled to a Royal Protection Officer, she is frightened of being mobbed or put upon. A travelling companion usually puts a stop to this but, of course, Sarah has to pick up the cost of two air fares.'

CHAPTER TWENTY
THE BIG D

Late one night, Sarah rang for a reading. As I lay out the cards, I said, 'Ah, ha! It's the marriage business.' Sarah asked me excitedly, 'Does that mean I'm going for the big D then? When? When? Tell me, Vasso, tell me. Is it soon?' As I continued the reading, the cards seemed to be telling me that a new man would enter her life and change everything, while another man, someone very close to her, but not her husband, would soon be leaving it.

'Oh good! I hope that means Number Three,' said Sarah, referring to John. 'I think he might just disappear. But the new man, tell me about him. If there was someone new in my life, it would explain a lot of things. I do hope that's true. Maybe there's a new Number Nine on the horizon,' she said referring to her former crush on John Kennedy Jr.

Press speculation about Andrew and Sarah continued and when, in August 1995, they had their first holiday together since their formal separation was announced more than three years earlier, some Royal commentators became convinced that the Duke and Duchess of York were heading for a reconciliation.

Days before flying out with their daughters for the six-day trip to southern Spain, Andrew and Sarah were pictured kissing and laughing as Sarah presided over a charity golf tournament in aid of the Motor Neurone Disease Association at Wentworth, just a stone's throw from her rented home, Kingsbourne. Andrew even raised a laugh after giving Sarah, who looked beautifully slim in a navy-and-stone patterned summer dress, a tender kiss and telling the crowd, 'We are not getting engaged, you know. In fact, we are already married.'

It was a typical display of affection that the public had again become accustomed to seeing. Sarah and Andrew were now regularly laughing and joking in each other's company, giving the impression that they really were the best of friends. This, of course, was very good news for the young princesses — nothing could be more important to young children than seeing their parents happy and relaxed together.

On 11 August, Andrew, Sarah and the girls travelled together to Farnborough military airfield in Hampshire, where a private jet was waiting to whisk them away.

Sarah, wearing a flowered dress, beamed as she shepherded the children up the steps of the aircraft, followed by Andrew who looked casual in sunglasses and a white shirt. To the outside world, all the signs pointed to one big, happy family.

If only they knew what I was about to learn.

Days after she returned from Spain, Sarah rang saying she had some very exciting news for me. Just as I had predicted, there was a new man on the scene who she hoped would play a part in her life. She had met him on the very holiday that many Royal commentators were claiming marked the start of her new life together with Andrew. It proved only how little these so-called experts really knew or understood Sarah. She and Andrew had been staying at Cazalla de la Sierra, a small village one hour north of Seville. The man, British but dark and mysterious and of gipsy origin, was giving painting lessons at a converted 17th century olive mill in the village. Sarah was bowled over by his work and, no doubt, by the fact that he was ruggedly good-looking. She had begged him to give her lessons, which he happily agreed to do.

Sarah was terribly excited about her new friend and rang for a reading as soon as she arrived home. 'There's someone new, Vasso, we'll call him "Gypsy". Tell me what the cards tell you about Gypsy,' she asked. 'You must tell me everything you can see. There is something really special about him.' Sarah told me that they had immediately hit it off and that she couldn't wait to see him again. 'He's so handsome, so dark and mysterious, I think I'm falling for him, Vasso.' I laughed out loud, saying: 'Here we go again!' Sarah giggled, 'I know, but it's so exciting.' Every time Sarah rang she would tell me about Gypsy — she never used his name on the telephone — and how they had been secretly meeting since their return to Britain and how he had been helping her with her painting.

I gave her my usual warnings about being careful and of not getting hurt, but I knew even as I spoke I was wasting my breath. One evening, Sarah rang me just after midnight to talk about Gypsy. 'I've fallen in love with him, Vasso. I don't know what I can do to stop myself,' she confided. 'But no one must know about him. He is terrified of people finding out and of all the publicity that would follow. He's a very private person. We've been spending an awful lot of time together and getting to know each other really well. He's so fascinating and has taught me so much.'

Over the following weeks, she began visiting him for art lessons at his home and she told me she had asked him out for dinner on a number of occasions, but he had always refused. The more he rebutted her advances, the harder she went after him. 'It's almost as if he's playing hard to get,' she told me. She said he was such a talented artist that she was going to make him rich and famous. 'What do the cards tell you about him, Vasso? Do you think he is going to be famous?'

I was somewhat amazed when, in early December 1995, Sarah told me she had given an interview to the *Sunday Telegraph* introducing her gypsy artist friend, whose name was Paul Gaisford, particularly as she had always stressed no one should find out about their friendship.

She used the magazine article to reveal how she had organised an exhibition of his work, apparently with the backing of Prince Andrew. She even posed for a photograph with Paul, sitting in the back of his Romany caravan. I got the impression that Paul seemed embarrassed as Sarah heaped praise on his paintings: 'His work is so good, people have got to see him. You can't talk about Paul's work in generalised terms as it is so diversified. But I like his use of light and I see huge depth and inspiration.'

It was so typical of Sarah's indiscretion. Instead of keeping their friendship away from the prying eyes of the newspapers, she had foolishly decided to go public, thereby inviting intense media speculation about the exact nature of their relationship. By publicly backing his exhibition, she thought she was doing him a favour when I believed the exact opposite was to be true.

Paul was a reclusive 54-year-old with a string of broken marriages and relationships behind him. He hated being in the limelight, but suddenly found teams of reporters camped outside his isolated Cotswold cottage in Bourton-on-the-Water, Gloucestershire, where Sarah had been a frequent visitor. Journalists began delving into his background, desperate to discover some dark secrets about the Marlboro-smoking gypsy artist with a taste for expensive shirts and French designer jackets. His water-colours of gypsy caravans and animals also came in for close scrutiny. I think Paul quickly realised the terrible mistake he had made in allowing himself to be bullied into staging an exhibition with the public backing of the Duchess. It was too late for him to do anything about it — the damage had already been done.

..................*

At the end of October 1995, Sarah decided to do something about all the talk of a reconciliation with Andrew and publicly fuelled speculation about a divorce in an interview with America's biggest selling magazine, *TV Guide*.

'My husband and I think the family unit is very important,' she told them. 'We may be separated, but we show up at weddings and events together. The children have to feel like they have a family. Why should they be caught in the middle? We're not divorcing them.' It was the first time Sarah had publicly mentioned a divorce and many interpreted her remarks as signalling an end to their marriage in the near future. Even if Sarah was thinking about divorce, I was convinced she would only go through with it if she was sure there was another man, and a very wealthy one at that, waiting in the wings to marry her.

During the interview, she spoke of her fondness for the American way of life: 'You have to give children praise and listen to them. Americans are better than the British at seeing what a child can do and enhancing the potential. My own mother called me vain whenever I looked at myself in the mirror and I used to do the same with Beatrice. But I've stopped doing that. A child gains confidence by being told she's pretty when she looks in the mirror.' Asked if Andrew supported her work writing the Budgie books, Sarah said, 'As long as my husband's happy, that's the main thing. He's very OK with Budgie. He's very supportive of me.' She said she had recovered from the bleak times during the early days of their separation, 'I stay positive,' she said. 'I wasn't during the early part of the separation, but now I try to see every day as wonderful. The trees are green and the air is good. I think it's important to take every day and enjoy it. Seize it. This is life.'

CHAPTER TWENTY-ONE
DIANORAMA

In late summer 1995, Sarah told me to expect a dramatic development concerning Diana, but I must admit I didn't appreciate just how dramatic that development would be. For almost a year, Diana and Sarah had been lunching together every Sunday — two young women who had married into Britain's Royal Family only to find themselves virtual outcasts when their marriages had failed, despite the fact that both believed their respective husbands were largely to blame. They were both 'outsiders', and when things had gone wrong, members of the Royal Household had closed ranks to protect the two Princes, leaving the 'outsiders' to fend for themselves. Both had suffered a great deal, but now they were older and wiser, each with two children to raise, and they talked of ways of exposing the Royal Family for what it was. The public should be made aware of what 'outsiders' had to go through, they decided, as they began to plot 'the master stroke'. Sarah said, 'She will do something that will send shock waves through the land.'

Sarah told me that Diana believed Charles would never be king. She believed something 'too terrible to even talk about' would happen to the heir to the throne. Once before he had come close to death after an avalanche in the Alps but Diana believed next time he might not be so lucky. It was in 1988 that Charles narrowly escaped death in an avalanche on the slopes of Klosters which killed his close friend Major Hugh Lindsay. After the tragedy, Princess Diana, who was with Charles on holiday, vowed never to return to the ski resort favoured by the rich and famous.

....................*

The BBC Panorama programme, watched by 100 million people world-wide, would stun Britain. Not only did Diana admit to having had an affair, she also doubted her husband's willingness, ability or even wish to become King and ruled herself out as ever being Queen, suggesting that Prince William might be the one to succeed his grandmother. Asked if she was in any way to blame for the fact that the role of the Monarchy was being openly discussed, Diana replied emphatically, 'No, I don't feel blame. Once or twice

I've heard people say to me that "Diana's out to destroy the Monarchy", which has bewildered me because why would I want to destroy something that is my children's future?'

In the run-up to recording the historic broadcast, Diana had discussed in great detail with Sarah and one or two other close advisers the role of the Monarchy and most of the other topics she had chosen to discuss. Diana was fully aware of the effect her broadcast would have, but she decided it was time to set the record straight so that people could judge for themselves what sort of a life she had had within the Royal Family.

Diana claimed that, as an innocent newlywed, she was thrown into the deep-end by Charles and forced to 'sink or swim'. Sarah told me she had felt exactly the same and the one person who should have been there for her, Andrew, had been nowhere to be seen. 'No marriage can work if the husband is never there to offer support when it is most needed,' Sarah added. 'Diana discovered that almost from day one. Charles was never there for her. For him, it was purely a marriage of convenience. He was under great pressure to marry and produce an heir and there was no way he could do that with Camilla. Diana was chosen not because Charles was in love with her, but simply because she was a suitable candidate. And when you are constantly in the public eye, with cameras watching your every move, it is a hundred times harder to make the marriage work. Papers begin to comment on the amount of time your husband is away and that brings it all home to you.'

Sarah always had one eye on the door marked 'D' for divorce, but during the interview Diana ruled out a complete end to her marriage insisting, 'I don't want a divorce.' She claimed she had never even discussed the subject, appearing to suggest the initiative should lie with Charles. 'I await my husband's decision of which way we are going to go,' she said.

Sarah particularly enjoyed Diana's vitriolic attack on those within the Royal Household who she believed saw her as a 'threat of some kind'. Asked why, Diana had replied, 'I think every strong woman in history has had to walk down a similar path and I think it's the strength that causes the confusion and the fear.' She said problems arose for her because 'I was the separated wife of the Prince of Wales. I was a problem. Full stop.'

Diana also revealed that she had been prevented from carrying out many public duties, something Sarah had encountered before her on many occasions.

Diana told how she was perceived as a liability, 'an embarrassment', she said. Visits abroad were blocked, mail was mislaid 'things that had come naturally my way' were stopped.

Sarah, excitedly sitting on the edge of a sofa at her

rented Surrey mansion, was among the millions who tuned in to watch the breathtakingly frank 55-minute interview with reporter Martin Bashir. But, unlike the masses glued to their screens, Sarah already knew what was coming for she was one of only a select handful of friends who had known in advance the magnitude of what Diana was about to reveal, having spent hours helping her carefully rehearse her answers in the weeks running up to the historic broadcast. Time and again, Diana attacked the arrogant coldness of the Royal Family and spoke of her sense of betrayal at her husband's love for the 'third person in our marriage', Camilla Parker-Bowles, and Sarah immediately picked up the telephone to congratulate her friend on a truly remarkable performance.

Sarah, who had been strong for Diana when she most needed her, and encouraged her to make the candid confessions that would plunge the Monarchy into its deepest crisis since Edward VIII put his love for a divorcee before the throne almost 60 years earlier, loved the broadcast. 'She did very well,' she told me. 'It's good that she told the truth and was so honest. I think it will also have done me some good as people will have a much clearer picture of the problems we've encountered. They can see what a dreadful lot they are.' The reference was pointed at those within the Palace who had made both their lives a misery. 'Some people at the Palace are still trying to make life as difficult as possible for Diana,' she added. 'I know it won't end here but at least now she's set the record straight. She wanted to let people judge for themselves.'

I asked Sarah if she had ever considered doing a similar interview to which she replied, 'Sometimes, but not now, not at the moment. I think people have got enough to think about now as it is.'

At the beginning of December, Sarah flew to New York to promote her book, *Budgie the Little Helicopter*, and spin-off toys and T-shirts. She was delighted at the success of the promotion at the famous Bloomingdale's department store in Manhattan, and with the reception she received from the American people. 'If the British people were as warm and friendly I'm sure my problems wouldn't be anywhere near as bad as they are,' she later told me. 'The Americans genuinely seem to like me.'

Thrilled at the success of her trip, she headed for Washington for a reception hosted by President Bill Clinton and his wife Hillary, where Sarah wore a beautiful set of jewels given to her as a wedding present by the Queen.

The following day, Sarah flew to New York's JFK Airport where she boarded a Heathrow-bound Concorde, leaving her dresser Jane Dunn-Butler — and the jewels — to catch a later British Airways flight.

Arriving back at Kingsbourne, Jane quickly realised

that some of Sarah's baggage had been tampered with and, to her horror, discovered that a diamond bracelet and matching necklace, together worth about £250,000, had been stolen. Privately Sarah was furious, especially on discovering that the jewellery had been stowed in the hold in an unlocked suitcase, but publicly she claimed she was 'pretty laid-back' about the episode and confidant they would turn up. She was particularly angry at newspaper headlines that lambasted her. 'Why do I get the blame for everything?' she asked me. 'The bag should never have been in the hold. It was nothing to do with me. It makes me so mad when everything is turned around to make it look like my fault.' It was also left to Sarah to ring the Queen and Prince Andrew to tell them about the theft.

Jane, who had worked for Sarah for more than seven years, was distraught. 'She was in a terrible state,' Sarah later told me. 'I think she felt as if her whole world had ended.' She said she had put her up at Kingsbourne for a couple of nights to show publicly that she was standing by her old friend.

There was enormous relief all round when the bracelet was found 24 hours later in a locker belonging to a 19-year-old New York baggage handler. The necklace, minus a few small diamonds, was later recovered at his home. 'What a relief! I was so lucky,' Sarah sighed. 'I remember your warning that something like this was going to happen. You were right as usual. I don't know why things like this always seem to happen to me. At least I don't think there's much else that could go wrong.' About nine months earlier, I had warned Sarah to be extremely careful when travelling with her jewellery, after I had seen a mishap involving a necklace during one of our readings. It never ceased to amaze me that Sarah was forever asking me for predictions, then totally ignoring the things I told her.

On 7 December, Sarah paid her annual visit to the East Surrey branch of the Motor Neurone Disease Association's Christmas party and appeared in buoyant mood as she chatted to victims and their carers. She handed over a signed painting of a landscape scene she had painted on her recent Spanish holiday. As she chatted to a 29-year-old man who had only recently been struck down by the muscle-wasting disease, Sarah suggested that he visit a faith healer. 'The Duchess said I should try it,' he later revealed. 'She said "you've got nothing to lose." She said you had to believe to make it work.' As Sarah left the party, she told waiting journalists that she was extremely pleased to be reunited with her stolen jewellery. 'I'm very relieved and very impressed with the security forces for finding them so quickly,' she said. Complimented on looking so trim, Sarah smiled and said, 'The secret of a good diet is to keep happy.'

CHAPTER TWENTY-TWO
'GEORGE'

It wasn't long before I learned that Sarah had given up her pursuit of Paul Gaisford and had become bored with the entire affair. I doubted they had actually been lovers; for if they had I expect Sarah would have told me. But from what she did tell me, however, I quickly realised she had lost all interest in the gypsy artist. 'I'll have to go through with the exhibition because of all the publicity, but I really can't be bothered any more,' she said. I asked if Paul was still keen to see her and she added, 'He's only around because of this exhibition, but after that he's going to have to crawl over hot coals to get near me.' So that was that, I thought. He had been a plaything, someone who had intrigued her for a short time, but now she was bored and wanted nothing more to do with him. So she was dropping him, returning him to the obscurity from which she had plucked him.

It was a typical example of a change I had noticed in Sarah over the years. She had grown more selfish, worrying only about herself and not about the people she called her friends. Sometimes she wouldn't ring me for weeks, then suddenly she would wake me in the middle of the night and beg me to do a reading there and then because she had something on her mind. She showed little consideration for me, wanting only to talk about herself and her problems. She would ask how I was and what I had been doing, but she never really listened to what I had to say.

..................*

The episode with the jewellery had left her downcast at yet another dose of bad publicity. She told me, 'It's been a difficult time. This country is terrible. It's hell! It really is a hellish country.' She felt that the Press couldn't wait for her to slip up again, and this left her feeling angry and annoyed.

Her affair with John was finally over for which Sarah was glad because 'he was so dangerous'. She asked me to do her a reading. I told her I could see a lot of jealousy around her from other women and there seemed to be another man in the cards, a very good-looking, middle-aged man who appeared to be extremely wealthy. 'Yes, yes, that's right,' she said excitedly. 'I don't know how you use those cards, but you are amazing. I think there is a new man around. I like the feel of him. He has beautiful dark eyes. And he's very rich.'

She told me he was 53 and an American. 'We'll call him "George",' she said. George was married but 'not very happily', judging by what she had seen of him and his wife when she had met them both the previous Sunday. 'Do you think he will be my new soul mate?' she asked. 'I have got this feeling that maybe he has fallen in love with me. I have with him. He's much better than the gypsy, I can tell you that.' I told her I could see travel in the cards and she asked, 'Do you think he will take me away from all this? He owns his own aeroplane so he could fly me anywhere. He's very rich. Do you think I am going to be with this man?' I could see the man had problems around him and Sarah was extremely relieved when I said they were emotional and not financial. 'Good, as long as he's got enough money to sort us out!' she joked.

She said she would see him in a few days time at a dinner, at which her husband and Diana would also be present. I told her she would have to look her best and she responded, 'I've already started looking at dresses today. I think I'll wear something in dark green or blue velvet. Those colours are so delicious.'

Sarah was travelling to New York the following week and she hoped he might call her while she was there. 'Perhaps this week he is just coming to look, to see what he thinks of me, and next week, well, who knows?'

She described him in detail, saying they had a great deal in common and the only thing she would have to change about him was his hair! 'I'd have to change his hair — it's blown dry with a hair-drier,' she laughed. 'We'd have to do something about that!' I told her this man was thinking of her and I would not be at all surprised if he asked her to join him on a trip. 'Do you think I could marry him?' she exclaimed. 'Perhaps I will even have a baby with him.'

I told Sarah to take one step at a time, 'You hardly know this man, how can you be saying these things already?' Sarah just responded: 'Oh, I just have one of my feelings, Vasso. I have very good feelings about this man.'

I asked about the jealousy I had seen in the cards and she said it was probably from his daughter. 'She's not very nice and she's jealous of me,' she said. 'Perhaps she is frightened of me taking her father away.' Sarah said he was well-known for his charity work and had already supported her with some of her business deals. She also told me that George was accompanied on his trip by a business manager called Barbara, who acted as a chaperone. 'Maybe he's told her about me,' said Sarah. 'I got on quite well with her, which could be very important.'

I asked Sarah what George did for a living, to which she replied: 'He is into so many different things, it's impossible to know exactly what he does. I don't know him very well yet, but let's hope that changes soon.'

I later discovered the name of the man Sarah had fallen in love with — a tycoon called Ray Chambers who was said to be notoriously publicity-shy. His personal fortune was estimated at £600 million and he was known in America as St Ray because of his extensive work for charity. Bonnie Brownlee, a spokeswoman for Sarah's New York-based charity, Chances for Children, told a Sunday newspaper, which inquired about their relationship, 'They've spoken about working together to help homeless and needy children.' I'm sure no one else could have had an inkling about Sarah's true feelings for St Ray!

Sarah had had a secret meeting with Ray during her recent visit to America, at which she told him of her worsening financial plight and asked if there was anything he could do, through his vast business contacts, to help her. They met up at Manhattan's Carlyle Hotel, where they were both staying in luxury suites. A photographer, who had seen them share a limousine back to the hotel, revealed, 'Sarah ducked when she spotted the camera and strode through a side door of the hotel. Seconds later, Chambers got out and went through the front door.' A cocktail waiter recalled serving drinks to the pair earlier that evening: 'She wanted a gin and tonic and I asked how she would like it. The Duchess replied "Straight in the vein".' Two days later, they both attended the Clintons' White House reception.

..................*

Sarah still had many financial problems. 'The most extraordinary thing is that for the first time in my life I'm not going skiing in January,' she said. 'I simply can't afford it.' Instead, the whole family was going to spend Christmas with the Queen and other members of the Royal Family at her Sandringham Estate in Norfolk. 'Andrew and the girls will stay in the big house and I'll stay in the little house,' she said. 'But I don't really mind because it means I will be able to get away by myself for a few days.' She wondered if there was any chance of 'George' taking her away. 'Maybe there will be a party going on somewhere and he will invite me,' she said. 'The Press will think I'm still at Sandringham so it's the only time I'll really be able to get away. It's a perfect time for me to go.'

Sarah had disclosed the fact that she was forsaking her annual skiing holiday while attending a function for the Motor Neurone Disease Association, of which she was both President and Patron. Not surprisingly, she didn't let on exactly why she wasn't going, but nevertheless it was seized on by the Press. Fergie missing her seasonal skiing jaunt? — Money must be tight, the newspapers alleged. I don't think any of them realised just how shaky the situation was for the Duchess.

I asked what Andrew would make of her new friend. 'Oh, he won't notice anything, he'll think it is just business,' she said. 'He's not going to like Andrew, is he?' She was concerned that if Ray liked Andrew he may think differently about her.

Sarah then left me open-mouthed by saying her husband had lots of girlfriends. She insisted 'he's a very naughty boy. Now it's me who's the good one. I don't do anything, but he does it all the time.' 'But doesn't he want you back, my baby?' I asked. 'Yes, he does. He says he wants me back, then he goes off with the girls,' she replied.

The conversation turned to Press speculation about Prince Edward's romance with Sophie Rhys-Jones, a blonde public relations consultant. 'She seems like a nice girl, do you think they will marry?' I asked her. Sarah made me laugh by spluttering, 'Oh, her!', and making a loud snorting noise. 'I really don't know. She doesn't look very nice, does she? She just tries to copy Diana the whole time.' She mocked Sophie as a 'Diana-clone' who tried to copy the Princess's hairstyle and fashion sense, even though Sophie had neither the looks nor the figure to carry it off. 'I don't know why she tries so hard, she should just be her own woman,' said Sarah. She and Diana spent hours discussing the woman who was widely tipped to become their sister-in-law. 'Blondie thinks it's quite funny how hard she tries to copy her,' Sarah said. Apparently, Diana felt quite smug whenever a newspaper carried pictures of the two women wearing similar outfits because she always outshone the younger Sophie. 'She says, "the poor girl just hasn't got it,"' added Sarah. I could detect some bitchiness in Sarah's tone and asked why she had got it in for Sophie. 'Everyone seems to be bending over backwards to protect her, they never did that for me,' said Sarah. 'But she'll discover what they're really like sooner or later. I don't mean to me nasty, Vasso, I'm just very tired. Perhaps things will be different for her. We'll just have to wait and see.'

....................*

Weeks later, Diana took William and Harry to visit Sarah at Kingsbourne. It was 17 December, the Sunday before Christmas, and over lunch Diana told the woman who had again become her closest friend and confidante that she had changed her mind about spending Christmas with the rest of the Royal Family, including Sarah, at Sandringham. 'She said she just couldn't go through with it,' Sarah told me later. 'She said it would be easier for everyone, except the boys, if she stayed away. I think she's planning to go abroad, somewhere hot for a few days. I can't say I blame her. She hates it up there anyway. She'll be far happier away from that lot.'

The next day Diana phoned the Queen to tell her of her intentions, explaining that it would be easier for everyone if she stayed away from the traditional Royal gathering. What I'm sure she did not expect was the handwritten letter from the Queen that arrived later that same day, suggesting it would be in her and Charles' best interests to seek a divorce as soon as possible. The letter came as a great shock to Diana, particularly as she had said during the Panorama interview that she had no wish to seek a divorce. Later that day, a letter arrived from Charles, saying he agreed with his mother that a divorce was now in their best interests. The screws were being turned, and Diana didn't like it one bit.

CHAPTER TWENTY-THREE
THOMAS MUSTER

After what Sarah described as a 'miserable' Christmas with the Royal Family at Sandringham, she was again off on her travels. 'I just need to get away for a while,' she told me. 'I think a break will do me good and allow me to recharge my batteries. I've had such a hectic time of late.'

First, there was a charity trip to Qatar in the Persian Gulf for the Mobil Tennis Open, during which she raised money for Children in Crisis. For many years, Sarah had been friends with the leading families in Qatar and several other fabulously wealthy Arab states and she loved the warmth and respect with which she was always greeted. She told me that more than anywhere else in the world, those countries always ensured she received hospitality befitting royalty. And there were always very generous and substantial donations for her charity, which was, after all, the reason for her visit. Sometimes Sarah hinted of an affair with a wealthy Arab, although she never revealed his name. She referred to him as 'White Dress' because of the traditional long, flowing Arab robes and would often ask during our readings: 'Tell me what you can see about White Dress in the cards. He's very handsome and very, very rich. Tell me if you can see him in my future, Vasso.' She would often dine alone with rich Arabs, as she loved their company and their impeccable manners. 'They're far better than English men, I can tell you that,' she said.

At the gala dinner marking the end of the tournament in Qatar, Sarah was pictured with Thomas Muster, a handsome Austrian tennis player who was ranked third in the world. The pair seemed to hit it off and the Press made much of the fact that they chatted and sipped champagne until almost three o'clock in the morning.

Sarah had been due to return home the following day, but at the last minute she cancelled her flight and instead boarded a plane to Sydney to visit her sister, Jane. I was surprised at the length of time Sarah had now been away, because it meant that Beatrice and Eugenie returned to school after the Christmas holidays without their mother there to ensure all went smoothly. She was usually so conscientious about taking the girls back to school herself after a holiday break and, although she phoned every night to say how much she was missing them and loved them dearly, I'm sure they must have been disappointed that she wasn't there.

Sarah explained that she had wanted to see Jane, who was five months pregnant, because she had experienced problems with previous pregnancies, including three miscarriages, and she wanted to offer her support. 'Jane was constantly on my mind and I had to see her,' Sarah said. 'I explained to the children I was going to see Aunty Jane and that was important for them, too, because they adore her. I believe that once I am away from my children, I might as well stay away for a bit longer rather than go home and then have to leave again. Although it may seem ludicrous to travel halfway around the world to spend just three nights with Jane, it makes perfect sense to me because I want to see how she is coping with the pregnancy. Being able to see Jane in person always makes me feel better. I think the most important thing we can give each other is support.'

The unscheduled visit was a wonderful surprise to Jane who had been craving family contact since learning she was pregnant with her second husband Rainer Leudecke's child. 'Sarah called me out of the blue and told me she was coming to see me,' said Jane, who has two children from her previous marriage. 'It was great knowing she would be here and we would be able to spend some time together.' The sisters spent hours catching up on lost time as they strolled along Sydney's sandy beaches and mixed with other shoppers in the bustling malls. Sarah also took the opportunity to indulge in her latest passion — painting watercolours. Jane told the Australian magazine *Woman's Day*: 'I think Sarah has felt wonderful being here because she's able to relax and be a normal person.' Sarah added, 'The most wonderful thing is to sit in the kitchen and have Jane make boiled eggs. This is the first time I have been alone with Jane since I was married ten years ago. Isn't that crazy! We've always had a tribe of children with us, too. We were always very close. Like all sisters there's a bond that cannot be broken, but we also have our disagreements. But if either of us has a problem, the other comes running. I don't know if I could ever live in Australia, although I love the country and the sunny skies and the people.' She said it would be particularly difficult returning to Britain because of the current 'misery' surrounding the Royal Family.

Jane revealed how they had been able to offer one another support and comfort during the 'bad times', and how hard it had been on Sarah when she left Britain to come and live in Australia 21 years earlier. 'She was just 15 and she had a rough time for a while trying to understand our parents' divorce,' said Jane. 'She was by herself for most of that time and it was very difficult. Our time apart has made us realise how important family is and we are definitely closer now than ever.'

Sarah persuaded Jane to fly to Melbourne for a night, so they bought their £250 return tickets and checked into the £170-a-night Regency Hotel. It didn't escape the attention of journalists that Sarah's new friend, Thomas Muster, had just flown to the city to prepare for the forthcoming Australian Open tennis championships. Jane insisted they had not met up with Muster: 'Sarah didn't even mention Thomas Muster's name. She was here to see me.' Of course that was untrue, and Sarah did manage to meet up with her handsome new friend. Why else would she have taken the trouble to fly all the way to Melbourne? And as for not mentioning his name to Jane, that would have been absolutely impossible for Sarah. Knowing her as I did, she would have been unable to stop herself talking about him, especially with her own sister who already knew her most intimate secrets.

Sarah, too, denied she had met up with the tennis star, claiming she and Jane had gone to Melbourne on a shopping expedition — a rather ludicrous claim, considering that Muster openly admitted he had invited Sarah to watch him practice. Muster, who was reported to be going through a bad patch with his long-time girlfriend, seemed a little embarrassed by the stories linking him with Sarah. 'She's charming, she's a lovely lady and we talked about lots of things,' he told reporters. 'We talked about fitness and training and skiing.' But he insisted there was no romance and stressed he had made daily calls to his 20-year-old girlfriend to reassure her that there was nothing between him and Sarah.

While romance may not have been on the tennis player's mind, I doubted the same could be said of Sarah. It was so typical of her to fall for someone at the drop of a hat. Handsome men always caught her eye. If they happened to be extremely rich as well, then so much the better.

The Press was intrigued by Sarah's sudden decision to fly to Australia, particularly because Muster was there and journalists at home were clamouring to know the true nature of their friendship. Unfortunately, Sarah had neglected to tell her trusted and well-respected Press spokeswoman Dominique Vulliamy about her spur-of-the-moment trip. Dominique found herself in the embarrassing position of having to admit to reporters that she knew nothing about the visit. When she did finally track Sarah down, Dominique was told to deny she had even been to Melbourne.

It was the final straw for Dominique who, in a heated exchange, asked Sarah how on earth she was supposed to protect her image if even she was kept in the dark about the Duchess's movements. She told her in no uncertain terms that the episode had been badly handled. Sarah flew home and straight into another row with Dominique, who told her she was not prepared to lie to the Press and that she must be crazy to think she could jet off here, there and everywhere without being spotted.

'If you don't like it, get out!' Sarah yelled. Dominique, who had been her mouthpiece for more than two years, didn't need to think twice. She told Sarah she had had enough and quit on the spot. Sarah was rather taken aback, immediately regretting what she had said. Dominique had been an excellent employee and, just as importantly, a good friend who had managed to turn public opinion in her favour against all the odds. Sarah was too headstrong to back down and by the time she had calmed down and realised what a stupid mistake she had made, it was too late. To add salt to the wound, Dominique's assistant Simone Canetty-Clarke walked out in support.

'There were tears on both sides,' a witness to this episode revealed. 'It all happened so quickly, it was awful.' Dominique refused to be drawn publicly, saying, 'I think I must keep things private. I don't want to say anything about what went on between me and the Duchess. That would be unprofessional of me. But I feel that a clean break now would be a good idea. I have enjoyed working for the Duchess, but now I feel it is time to move on.'

Dominique and Sarah had clashed many times in the past, but over the previous two months things had gradually been coming to a head. One friend said, 'They have clashed over a whole range of issues about how the Duchess sees her future and how she leads her life. There have been fundamental disagreements and it just couldn't go on. I don't know why but Sarah seems to end up like this with so many of the people who work for her. Leaving was the last thing that Dominique wanted to do, but the situation between her and the Duchess had become not only impossible but increasingly bitter. The biggest problem was that Sarah had just gone out of control leaving her staff wondering "what next?". The Duchess was spending more and more time popping up all over the place, deceiving people about the amount of money she owed and in disagreements with almost everybody. Dominique felt she couldn't cope without being informed about exactly what was going on. Against everybody's expectations Dominique was actually achieving, for the first time in ages, a decent Press for the Duchess. She was working all hours to do this without too many thanks. Instead, she realised she was about to be fired so she quit.'

There was also speculation about growing pressure on Sarah to cut back on the top-heavy staffing of her office. Her huge staff bill was something that troubled Sarah a great deal but she always told me, 'I'd cut back if I could but I just don't see how I can. There's such an incredible workload that, if anything, I could do with more help, not less.' Before Dominique and her assistant left, her staff wage bill amounted to £384,000 a year.

Somehow the Press got wind of Sarah's deepening financial crisis and the day after Dominique left, many newspapers carried front-page reports that she was more than £1m in debt.

I was one of the few people, outside the bankers and accountants, who knew the true figure was nearer £2m.

Sarah had told me so many times that she was cutting back on expenses and taking fewer holidays because she didn't have the money. Then, the next moment, she was jetting off halfway round the world to see her sister in Australia.

Sarah always decided she would sort her financial problems out tomorrow. Just one more trip, then she would tighten the purse strings. But the extravagance greatly concerned her bankers at the Royal bank of Coutts & Co, so much so that senior executives had made several appointments with Sarah to discuss ways of easing her worsening financial situation.

Just 12 months earlier, it had been revealed that Sarah was forced to leave a store without her shopping after staff insisted they needed authorisation for her Visa credit card, which had exceeded its limit. She left £105 worth of toys on the counter of the Reading branch of WH Smith while she went to her car to collect her cheque book.

In the summer of 1995, Sarah spent more than £50,000 on twelve formal dresses by the Danish designer Isabel Kristensen, while, at the same time, making arrangements to fly first-class with her daughters for a holiday in Bermuda. She also spent more than £3,000 on 20 pairs of boots and shoes in an afternoon's shopping spree at an upmarket boutique on New York's Fifth Avenue. It was also revealed that her phone bill, one of her largest extravagances, topped £4,000 a quarter.

Sarah was horrified that newspapers were carrying stories of her £1m debt but, tellingly, she didn't deny them. She was also greatly embarrassed that the papers were saying the Queen and Andrew were 'deeply concerned' at the size of her debts, mainly because it was true. Andrew was in no position to bail Sarah out of her financial quagmire, and Prince Philip would never have allowed the Queen to help out, even if she had wanted to do so.

One courtier said, 'It's a very worrying problem. Quite simply, the Duchess of York is massively in debt. The powers that be at Buckingham Place — I'm talking of the Queen and the Duchess's husband, Prince Andrew — know exactly what is going on and are very concerned. They believe the Duchess and her spending habits have become a runaway train. She spends a lot of money, and things have got totally out of control.' Another friend said, 'Sarah loves the good life, but I'm afraid she hasn't the income to match her tastes. She loves travelling and entertaining, but both are expensive pastimes.'

Sarah responded to the reports by saying, 'The truth is I am making financial cutbacks, huge ones. But the state of my financial accounts is not anyone else's business. I don't know other people's financial accounts so why should they know mine? It is not in the public interest. If someone wants to write that I am £1m in debt that is up to them. But nobody can say that I use any of my charity money for personal use because it would simply not be true. The truth is I always pay my own way.'

Sarah took her fund-raising very seriously and it worried her that people might not donate to Children in Crisis because of her own financial straits. 'Everything is just too horrible for words,' she told me. 'Of course I'm badly in debt, but who on earth leaks this information to the newspapers. It is none of their business.'

I asked Sarah how she was feeling and she told me, 'Dreadful, just dreadful. It's just these chips (money), it's been such a long time but there's still no sign of them. I'm very down, very disappointed, I just can't seem to do anything any more.'

The following day brought more anguish for Sarah when newspapers claimed the true extent of her debt was, in fact, nearer £3m and, unless she managed to turn around her fortunes soon, she could face bankruptcy. The amount of her overdraft was exaggerated but not by much and it terrified Sarah that so many of her personal affairs were being made public.

There was also an unprecedented statement from Buckingham Palace saying the Queen would not bail Sarah out of her financial crisis. It read: 'The Queen has made a generous provision to the Duchess of York over a number of years. Management of her financial affairs is the Duchess's responsibility.'

It was a humiliating blow to Sarah who was as astonished as anyone that the Queen had made a public statement about her financial affairs. Sarah, who was convinced Prince Philip was behind the move, was also furious that journalists had discovered that the Queen had bailed her out in the past, including the time in April 1994 when Coutts had ordered her to pay £500,000 within 14 days. The Queen had also helped Sarah out two years prior to that when she separated from Andrew.

Asked if the Queen would help clear Sarah's overdraft, a Palace spokesman added, 'No. These are matters which the Duchess of York must resolve with her bankers and other financial advisers. Her business ventures are conducted quite separately from any Royal duties and any transactions resulting from them must be resolved between the Duchess and her business associates and creditors. They are not a matter for the Queen.' Despite the tough stance, senior aides stressed the Queen would not allow the young Princesses Eugenie and Beatrice to suffer and there would always be adequate provision for them.

A member of Sarah's staff at Kingsbourne leaked a memo to the Press in which she had instructed them to keep within a strict new budget of £24,000 a month. The breakdown was as follows: rent, £6,000; entertainment and leisure, £8,000; clothes and shoes, £3,000; food and wine, £3,000; laundry, £2,000; and a further £2,000 for the children's expenses. This meant that her spending for the year, in the unlikely event that she managed to keep within her budget, was £288,000! That was excluding her quarterly telephone bill, which was usually about £4,000. Newspapers reported that Sarah spent more in a week than a lone parent with two children received in income support for a whole year. Not surprisingly, there was little sympathy for her plight.

I wondered what Sarah could do to ease her problems and was astounded when she told me she was flying to America on Concorde for a charity event. 'Everything's just too awful for words,' she complained. 'I've got some very important meetings that could be my only chance of getting out of this dreadful mess. I want you to beam in and tell me if you think it's going to be a successful trip. This is my last chance, Vasso.' The cards told me 'the chips' were not very far away and I told Sarah the good news. 'Oh, I do hope you're right, Vasso,' she said. 'It's about time I got some chips. I've waited so long. Sometimes I think they're never going to come.'

It was almost inevitable that the Press would discover that Sarah was taking the most expensive form of transport to America and the papers took great pleasure in reporting that 'hard-up Fergie' was also planning to take her daughters and their nanny, pushing the bill for flying by Concorde to more than £9,000. Sarah had little option but to re-arrange her plans, booking her party instead on a scheduled British Airways 747.

Sarah could not have taken the trip at a worse time. Instead of lying low for a few weeks and escaping the headlines, she decided she could not let people in America down as the trip included an important charity event that had been arranged months in advance. More importantly, she had arranged to meet a group of rich American businessmen who offered the only possible way out of her financial crisis.

So, determined as always to hold her head high, she went to America, accompanied by a plane-load of journalists who would monitor her every move. During the flight, Sarah agreed to spend a few minutes with representatives of the Press, believing it would give her a chance to set the record straight. Echoing Diana's words from the *Panorama* interview, Sarah told them: 'I am concerned that perhaps I have enemies within the Palace who may be behind the stories that have appeared this week.' She added, 'I am going to be strong. I have got to be strong. I will not let them get me down. But I can tell you that the figures quoted in the Press concerning my debts are exaggerated. They are inaccurate.' She refused to be drawn on the precise amount of her debts, but replied, 'Life goes on and I have to do the best I can. Life is not gossip or tittle-tattle, it is the air we breathe and being nice to people.'

Sarah was already tired and drained and knew it would be an uncomfortable trip as the eyes of the world were on her. Surprise had also been expressed at her decision to take her daughters away during school time, which also meant that taxpayers had to pick up a bill for several thousand pounds for their two Royal Protection Squad officers. Much was made of the fact that she had booked into a £500-a-night suite at one of Washington's leading hotels. Many wondered exactly what Sarah had meant when she said she was making serious cut-backs.

Some considered it just as extraordinary that she planned to meet up with her former lover Steven Wyatt and his wife, Cate. Sarah was having talks with officials from the international fund-raising organisation the Millennium Society, of which Cate was co-Chairman. The news didn't surprise me in the slightest. Sarah still cared a great deal for Steven and always looked forward to their occasional telephone calls, although they were far less frequent now. She knew meeting him would open up old wounds, but this wouldn't stop her meeting the man who had stolen her heart a few, short years ago.

The Press also managed to track down the now elusive John Bryan who stuck up for Sarah, rubbishing reports that her debts were anywhere near as high as £3m. He told them, 'Her debt facility is a perfectly appropriate facility and is one in which she has in relationship with her bank. It's a long-established relationship and I don't see any problem with it and I think it is being overplayed in terms of its importance. I don't think she needs any bail out. She has secured her debts and is in perfectly good standing with the bank. It is much ado about nothing, frankly. She's a writer, she has got many projects in the pipeline and I am sure she will do very well with all of them.'

Sarah flew to New York where one of her first meetings was with Ray Chambers, who would turn out to be the 'white knight' Sarah had been searching for. Ray, a notoriously secretive man, was said to be one of the main backers behind a deal that wiped out her debts. It was a tremendous relief for Sarah and she couldn't hide her delight as she turned up for a charity dinner that evening, smiling broadly and looking as if she didn't have a care in the world.

A spokesman for the Duchess revealed, 'We are pleased to announce that, following detailed discussions over recent weeks, an agreement has been reached which provides a solid base for the activities of HRH the Duchess of York and ensures the payment of creditors. The agreement has the support of Coutts & Co.'

The agreement was cautiously welcomed by the Palace. A spokesman called it a 'welcome development' and said that the Queen was 'delighted'. There was some concern as to the exact terms of the deal and the Palace spokesman said they would be examining it very carefully.

Sarah refused to be drawn on the deal that had been struck, saying she was in New York on charity business. 'We started over here a year ago and we are doing well,' she said, adding that she had brought Beatrice, seven, and Eugenie, five, because she wanted to show them a 'new culture'. She said, 'I wanted to make them appreciate what they have got and how lucky they are. I want to show them interesting things and open their eyes.'

She revealed that she had asked both the girls to give up their favourite Christmas presents so they could be sent to needy children in the former Yugoslavia: 'They didn't hesitate in handing over their Barbie dolls. It's important in life to give and take. They are learning. The most important thing for me is to be able to help children find a better life. That's why I'm here.' She also added, 'I love New York. I love the people — they are so positive.'

CHAPTER TWENTY-FOUR
HOW SHE BLEW IT

If Sarah thought that was the end of her money problems, she was wrong. Just a week after sewing up the American deal she found herself in the embarrassing situation of facing a High Court writ over a £100,000 debt. Her former friend, the Indian-born society hostess Lily Ratham Mahtani, claimed she had lent Sarah the money to enable her to take a six-week holiday with her daughters in the South of France in August 1994. She claimed Sarah had promised to repay the money after a 'reasonable period' yet when she had asked for the money six months later, Sarah had repaid just £5,000.

It could not have escaped Mrs Mahtani's notice that the woman who owed her nearly £100,000 had managed to pull off a deal on her latest American jaunt that was said to have wiped her slate clean. The two women had fallen out over the debt and, although Mrs Mahtani was said to be fabulously wealthy and lived in a luxurious Mayfair home, she, like many others, had just decided that Sarah had taken her for a ride for long enough. She told one of her closest friends, 'I lent her the money in good faith and I didn't expect to be treated like this. I was assured the money would be returned but little has happened.' The friend also revealed that she had agonised for nearly a year before deciding she had no option but to take legal action. It was a devastating blow to Sarah who had returned happy and triumphant from America, believing the worst was now behind her. It was also seen as heaping humiliation on Buckingham Palace, as it was revealed that Sarah was the first member of the Royal Family to be pursued through the courts over an outstanding debt. Ironically, the writ was filed as Sarah enjoyed a three-and-a-half-hour lunch at a swish London restaurant.

She was given just 14 days to repay the money, file a defence or ignore it and risk having the bailiffs knock at her door. Needless to say, Sarah immediately instructed her lawyers to deal with the matter.

It seemed quite incredible to me that Sarah had borrowed such a large sum of money from a woman who could hardly have been considered a close friend in the first place. It also demonstrated just how extravagant she had been at a time when her finances were in such dire straits. Instead of tightening her purse strings, Sarah spent £20,000 on renting a villa near Cannes on the Côte d'Azur and tens of thousands more living life to the full. It was so typical of Sarah. She wanted to be seen as a woman of great wealth, someone for whom nothing was too expensive or too extravagant. Cases of champagne, costing up to £60 a bottle, were delivered almost daily as Sarah threw lavish parties for the rich and famous. She revelled in the role of party hostess and mingled with Andrew Lloyd Webber and his wife Madeleine, Roger Moore, Sir David Frost, Robert Sangster, the millionaire race horse owner, and pop star Belinda Carlisle. At one stage she had even decided to ask John to fly over and join her, but was wisely persuaded that just two years after the infamous toe-sucking scandal it was, perhaps, just a little too risky. She still spent hours on the telephone to John, saying how much she missed him and how she wished he was there to share the fun. As soon as she put the phone down, Sarah would ring me for a reading.

Guy Hoffer, the caretaker at the Cannes villa, described how, 48-hours before she arrived, two of her staff turned up to check everything was in order. 'They went out and bought an extra washing machine, spin drier, cooker and two extra beds for the bodyguards,' he recalled. 'A truck came from England with sun loungers and swimming-pool toys for the children. Just before she arrived, the bodyguards checked all the rooms, turning out my drawers and cupboards to see if there was a camera. I didn't have a camera, but they wouldn't take my word for that.' Five extra telephones were installed, including one at the poolside. Her arrival was like a 'whirlwind'. Hoffer added, 'One girl did nothing but look after the flowers. Every day they spent about £200 on flowers for displays around the pool, on the terraces and in the villa. She didn't behave like a Duchess, all her staff sat down for meals with her, which I thought was strange for a member of the Royal Family. There were huge buffet tables of food, and a full English breakfast every morning. Everyone sat down for afternoon tea and dinner was at 11 p.m. Much of the champagne was opened and never finished. There was a great deal of waste, but everyone had a great time until around four in the morning. I would get up around seven to clean up with her staff. The Duchess usually got up around 11.30 and would go around saying good morning to everyone. Once, she asked me about my life and said she was not very happy because she did not get on with her in-laws. I told her that was the same for a lot of people.'

Sarah's financial troubles continued to worsen. A member of staff rang to warn her that the Electricity Board was threatening to cut off her supply because of an unpaid bill for £1,400. Sarah had refused to sign any cheques before leaving for her holiday, telling staff, 'I don't want to sign any cheques. I'm not interested.'

Lily Mahtani was not the only creditor to come forward. Sarah Beni, manager of the Wentworth Hair and Beauty Salon, revealed that the Duchess had neglected to pay her for two home visits and she was owed the princely sum of £40! 'We were talking about the Duchess's debts and it made me laugh because I suddenly remembered she owed me money,' she said. 'I was called to the house last September and October but never got paid. The bill is around £40 — but I think I'll probably write it off now!'

Sarah's money troubles refused to go away. Weeks later, the hire firm from which Sarah rented much of her furniture threatened to take her to court, claiming she owed thousands in unpaid rent. Accountants from Room Service Designs sent a warning letter and invoice advising Sarah that she had fallen behind with her payments for the furniture she had taken with her from her previous home at Romenda Lodge. Among the items Sarah rented in a package costing £600 a month were an antique mahogany dining-table, a yew bookcase for the children's playroom, a writing desk, occasional tables and a three-seater sofa with matching chair.

Yet again, there was the threat of bailiffs knocking at the door and taking away other furniture to make good the debt. It was seen as a humiliating sign that creditors were losing patience with the Duchess, who was reported to have just struck a deal worth £3m.

Among those who had taken particular interest in Sarah's highly publicised American dealings was John Bryan, who believed he was due a share of any deals concerning the marketing of Sarah's cartoon helicopter, Budgie. John, struggling with major financial problems of his own, was furious that he had not been consulted about the deal and immediately instructed his lawyers in Germany to find out all they could. The threat of legal action from John raised the extraordinary prospect of Sarah having to appear before a German court and threatened to throw into the public arena more intimate details of how their business and personal relations had been so intricately entwined.

John claimed he had been responsible for turning around the fortunes of the Budgie cartoon and had struck a deal with Sarah that entitled him to a ten per cent share of global earnings. He also claimed that Sarah had promised him a third of all her earnings from Budgie's TV, film and book publishing rights. He claimed that, without his support, Budgie would never have been a success: 'That property was totally dead when I got hold of it. It had no credibility, nobody would deal with it, nobody would touch it with a ten-foot pole. It had been wiped out because of the bad deals that had been done. The publishers turned it down after they had produced a book because it was too much of a pain in the neck. They had blown it, they had blown the property.'

He claimed that he had saved Budgie from disaster by clinching the deal with Sleepy Kids in July 1994: 'I think it made the owners of that company $20m (£13m). The stock was 5p when I did the deal and it went up to 125p as one of the highest earners on the entire stock market.' He said he was unable to put an exact figure to his claims, adding, 'No one knows at this stage what has been received and what the contracts state. Really, the bottom line is cash.' And cash, at that precise moment, was what John desperately needed. He claimed he had a verbal agreement with Sarah about the marketing of Budgie and he expected her to honour it. 'I'm quite certain that at the end of the day, when push comes to shove, there's no reason not to do the right thing,' he said. 'I'm sure she will.'

It was a clear threat to Sarah to pay up or risk fighting him through the courts. John believed Sarah's biggest problem was that he knew her too well. One of life's born gamblers, he figured the last thing Sarah would want was a long and costly legal battle in which she would inevitably be the loser no matter what the financial outcome. He said, 'A lot of people have been pushed to the limit. Everyone has their limits. She has certainly pushed people to the bitter end.' Michael Korde, a member of his German legal team, added, 'I have had numerous telephone conversations with Mr

Bryan and can confirm we are trying to get money from the Duchess of York. It is possible that if we get nowhere Mr Bryan will bring legal proceedings in Germany and the Duchess might be asked to give evidence.'

John, however, was about to lose the first round of his gamble. Sarah made it clear she had no intention of giving him money she did not believe he was owed. After a lengthy meeting with legal and financial advisers, Sarah issued a terse statement though her personal assistant, Kate Waddington, saying, 'The Duchess of York denies absolutely any agreement with Mr Bryan concerning the prospective income from her cartoon character Budgie. She will, therefore, defend vigorously any proceedings which Mr Bryan might choose to initiate on the subject.'

In simple terms, the gloves were off. It was the first public admission that they were no longer on good terms — a clear sign to everyone that the once inseparable pair had finally gone their separate ways.

Sarah was making it clear she believed she had already paid back John's financial investment in setting up the original deal with Sleepy Kids. She was prepared to fight him through the courts to defend her stance.

Over the years I had warned Sarah time and again that the relationship would end in tears and here, finally, was the proof. It had always been obvious to me that John had been out for whatever he could get. From the outset, he hoped his connections with British Royalty would open doors and allow him to do deals which would give him the fabulous wealth of which he had always dreamed. But it had all gone wrong, one by one the doors had been firmly slammed in his face until even Sarah had shut him out of her life.

Now he was clutching at straws. I believed that by threatening court action he was trying to force Sarah's hand, convinced she would back down rather than risk a potentially humiliating battle through the courts. It seemed to me that Sarah was calling John's bluff. She knew John had a string of creditors chasing him for cash and was probably gambling on the fact that a costly legal fight was the last thing he would want.

The following day it was revealed that a top European bank had laid a £900,000 fraud charge against John in Germany. It alleged he had borrowed the money to prop up his ailing German construction company, on the strength of his claims of having a contract entitling him to a percentage of future earnings from Sarah's Budgie books. Following the collapse of his company, the money was never repaid. A spokesman for the Frankfurt prosecutor's office revealed, 'Theoretically, under German law, Mr Bryan could face a maximum of five years in jail if found guilty. The bank doesn't know if the contract was genuine or if Mr Bryan got any money from it. But they feel they were deceived and this is why they have laid a charge.' John's German lawyer, Dr Achin Groepper, confirmed the charges: 'That's correct, I know all the facts and it is serious.'

More worryingly for Sarah, Dr Groepper raised the prospect that John was now willing to spill the beans and sell his account of their four-year relationship. 'We have a lot of things to discuss and this could include John giving his story,' he said.

At the same time, in London, Sarah decided to fight Mrs Mahtani's writ demanding the return of her £100,000 'loan'. Her lawyers waited until the last moment to inform the High Court that she wanted another 14 days to prepare a file in defence of the action. A source close to Sarah revealed, 'She will be having some important discussions with lawyers over the next few days to decide on what action to take to resolve the matter. At the moment she is under immense pressure trying to deal with legal actions by Mrs Mahtani as well as Mr Bryan.' It now seemed inevitable that, if she did press ahead and defend the action, she would almost certainly have to appear in court, thus making her the first member of the Royal Family to give evidence in the High Court.

John was also facing the threat of further legal action. In July 1994, he was ordered to pay £55,000 to Sarah's sister Jane and her husband Rainer Luedecke after arranging coverage for them of their wedding in

Hello! magazine. The couple brought a High Court action claiming that John had breached his duty while acting on their behalf. Kathryn Garbett, the couple's solicitor, said, 'We brought an action against John Bryan for recovery of monies received by him from *Hello!* magazine. Mr Bryan was acting for Mr and Mrs Luedecke at the time and we said that he had breached his duty to them.'

It was that action which, on 7 August, 1996, led to John being declared bankrupt in England. London's High Court heard he had still failed to repay the couple's £30,000 costs from a court action over the 1994 wedding photographs. It was also revealed he owed £15,646 to American Express and £9,476 to London solicitors Penningtons. After a twenty-minute private hearing, Kathryn Garbett said, 'We are very pleased with the outcome. Mr Bryan had over six months to settle his obligation to meet his clients' costs. He is solely responsible for the predicament in which he now finds himself. We will be co-operating fully with the trustee appointed by the Court to secure his assets worldwide.' Newspapers reported that the search for assets was likely to concentrate on America, where John, 40, was living.

Meanwhile, there had been more humiliation for Sarah who had been banned from using the Queen's Palace mail service free of charge and was no longer able to take Royal Squadron flights. She saw the walls closing in on her from every side and it left her very, very frightened.

..................*

Sarah had been closely following Thomas Muster's progress on the tennis circuit and had kept in regular touch by telephone. On 16 February, 1996, he slipped into Britain for a secret rendezvous with Sarah. Because of the continued Press speculation about their friendship, a statement was issued on her behalf, saying: 'It is well known the Duchess and Thomas Muster are good friends.' But Sarah refused to be drawn further on the matter.

This meeting was deeply upsetting for Muster's long-time girlfriend Mariella Theiner, who publicly told Sarah to cool the relationship. 'She has two children, she should stay at home and stop running around the world to see my boyfriend. She may be attracted to Thomas but I doubt he is attracted to her. She is too ugly for him. I am younger and prettier. I don't know why she does it.' Asked if she had questioned him about the relationship, Mariella, the daughter of a wealthy insurance underwriter, replied, 'I can't talk to him, he's playing tennis. Why don't you ask the Duchess if it's true? She's a great woman for having affairs; there was all that business with John Bryan so it's difficult to know what she's up to. After the first rumours, I asked Thomas what was going on and he assured me everything was made up. I want him to look me in the eyes because I don't believe he would lie to me. Thomas can be absolutely sure that I do not love him for material reasons. I do not need his money. I am rich and spoilt myself.'

As the days passed and there was still no word from her boyfriend, serious doubts began to be cast in Mariella's mind. She asked one journalist, 'Do you know if this rumour about him seeing the Duchess is true? It isn't, is it? He is the love of my life, and I believe I am for him, too. At least I think so. If these stories about Fergie are true I would like to think about it. I would like to hear his reasons for it. But in any case I would not compete with Fergie. Our relationship was built on love and trust. It would hurt very much if it ended.'

It was not long before their relationship did end. The poor girl grew sick to the teeth about the speculation and exasperated at the way the man she loved had foolishly been taken in by Sarah. I felt very sorry for Mariella. Muster was just another one of Sarah's playthings — another rich and famous man with whom she had quickly become infatuated, no doubt with one eye on his considerable bank balance. I could see in the cards that there was no future for them and wondered whether Sarah had given a second's thought to the fact she was responsible for destroying a happy and loving relationship. Probably not, I thought, all that seemed to matter to Sarah was her own well-being and happiness. Other people were there to be trampled. If there was any blame cast in her direction she would shrug it off, saying she couldn't be held responsible for Muster falling for her. As far as Sarah was concerned, *nothing* was ever her fault.

CHAPTER TWENTY-FIVE
THE DIVORCE

I learned that Sarah and Andrew were to divorce shortly after a statement was issued to the Press Association News Agency by the couple's lawyers on 16 April, 1996. Almost immediately journalists began ringing me and everyone else who had ever been connected with Sarah or Andrew, eagerly seeking inside information on the latest Royal divorce. I said I was very sad, but had nothing further to add.

The divorce broke in newsrooms across the country with a simple statement at 4.51 p.m. saying: 'PA NEWSFLASH: DUKE AND DUCHESS OF YORK ARE TO DIVORCE, ACCORDING TO JOINT STATEMENT BY THEIR SOLICITORS.' A few minutes later, the full statement was issued. It read:

THE DUKE AND DUCHESS OF YORK

ANNOUNCED THROUGH THEIR RESPECTIVE SOLICITORS, HENRY BOYD-CARPENTER OF MESSRS FARRER & CO AND DOUGLAS ALEXIOU OF MESSRS GORDON DADDS, THAT THEY HAVE AGREED, AFTER MORE THAN TWO YEARS' SEPARATION, THAT THEIR MARRIAGE SHOULD FORMALLY BE ENDED. ACCORDINGLY THE NECESSARY LEGAL PROCEEDINGS ARE UNDER WAY AND IT IS ANTICIPATED THAT THE DECREE ABSOLUTE WILL BE MADE AT THE END OF MAY.

'THE DECISION BY THE DUKE AND DUCHESS IS A PERSONAL ONE, AND THEIRS ALONE. HER ROYAL HIGHNESS THE DUCHESS OF YORK HAS CHOSEN NOT TO USE THE STYLE "HER ROYAL HIGHNESS" AND WILL CONTINUE TO BE THE DUCHESS OF YORK. AT THE EXPRESS WISH OF THE DUKE AND DUCHESS AND IN THE INTERESTS OF THEIR CHILDREN, WHICH THEY REGARD AS OF PARAMOUNT IMPORTANCE, NO FURTHER STATEMENT WILL BE MADE OR INFORMATION PROVIDED. CONSISTENT WITH THE STATEMENT MADE BY THE BUCKINGHAM PALACE PRESS OFFICE ON 28 JUNE 1993 THE CHILDREN WILL CONTINUE TO LIVE WITH THE DUCHESS, AND BOTH PARENTS WILL PARTICIPATE FULLY WITH THEIR UPBRINGING.

The Queen had been informed and was said to be 'saddened' by the decision, which came just days before her 70th birthday.

To my mind, a lot of things just didn't add up. I hadn't spoken to Sarah for many weeks, her phone calls having suddenly stopped as they had done on a number of occasions over the years. The last time we talked, Sarah had asked me to be by the telephone early the following morning as she was desperate for a reading about something 'extremely' important. She seemed extremely uptight so I cancelled several of my day's appointments and waited patiently for her call. It never came. Sarah could be so infuriating.

With hindsight, Sarah must have been under enormous pressure at the time to agree to a divorce. I knew it was not what she wanted and wondered what deals must have been struck for her to agree to something she had so long resisted. Of course she had given a lot of thought to the matter over the four years since the official separation, but she was relatively happy with the way things were. Sarah liked being the wife of Prince Andrew, even if they were estranged, knowing it offered her a degree of protection and security that would be swept away once she became his ex-wife. As the wife of the Queen's second son she could not be treated in the cavalier manner she would undoubtedly now be subjected to by the Palace courtiers whom she knew detested her. For them, it was a victory; for Sarah, it was as if she had been knifed in the back.

Sarah had often told me she would only agree to a divorce on her terms and, usually with a laugh, only if she was one hundred per cent sure there was a new, rich husband waiting in the wings, which certainly wasn't the case at this time. Being forced into a divorce was the one thing she dreaded more than anything else and I knew she would be devastated.

It also surprised me greatly that Andrew had agreed to a divorce as he had told me many times how he hoped for an eventual reconciliation with Sarah, who he still loved. To him, it was a distant dream, but still a possibility and I'm positive a divorce was the last thing he really wanted.

I also knew that the claim that Sarah had *chosen* to drop the title 'Her Royal Highness' had to be untrue. Whenever we spoke she had always stressed how important being an HRH was to her, not least because she felt it gave her the respect she believed was her due as a member of the Royal Family. Sarah told me of her fury when a woman had refused to address her as Your Highness and had failed to bow or curtsy on being introduced at a recent charity event. 'Can you believe the nerve of the woman?' Sarah asked. 'I was helping her charity and yet she refused to show me the slightest bit of respect. I find it quite incredible someone could be so rude.' It was a typical example of just how precious the title was to Sarah. She knew it had opened doors for her across the world — there was no way she would have given it up lightly. Sarah had obviously been forced into a corner. She had been out-manoeuvred and stripped of the title that gave her the status she craved.

It was also agreed that there would be a relatively small financial settlement for Sarah, in addition to the £2m agreed at the time of the separation. Sarah knew the extra £500,000 she would receive was as much as she could expect. She was well aware she had pushed her luck too far in the past and her pride would not allow her to go back to the Queen, cap in hand, to beg for more, although she could, of course, use the money. She knew the Family would always ensure her daughters, Beatrice and Eugenie — fifth and sixth in line to the throne — would never want for anything. The Queen, who I'm sure would have appreciated Sarah's lack of demands, loved the girls a great deal and more than adequate provisions would always be made for them.

Andrew would continue to receive £249,000 a year from the Queen to fund his living expenses and Royal duties, as well as drawing his Royal Navy salary of £30,544. He would continue to pay for the girls' schooling and help to bear some of Sarah's costs for renting Kingsbourne.

The whole issue of the divorce troubled me a great

deal. There were just too many pieces that didn't fit together. It seemed to me that Sarah and Andrew were getting divorced not because it suited them, but because it suited others like Prince Philip who I'm sure must have bullied the Queen, as he so often did, into believing a divorce was best for the sake of both their son and daughter-in-law. The truth was he didn't give a damn about Sarah or how 'the system' she hated and had been so unable to cope with, had chewed her up and was now spitting her out. As far as he was concerned it was 'good riddance' and the sooner Princess Diana followed her the better.

What saddened me so much was that Andrew and Sarah were as close as they had ever been. Sarah and the girls were in the middle of a week-long skiing trip in Verbier, Switzerland — ironically, staying at the home of former love Paddy McNally — when the announcement was made. On the ski slopes, she admitted to journalists that it was 'the saddest day of my life' but that she and Andrew remained the 'bestest of friends'. Still wearing her wedding ring, she added, 'I take every day as it comes. Every day is a new day. I spoke to Andrew today, I speak to him every day. I am feeling very well and the children are very well. The Duke is very well. We are all very well.' She intimated nothing would change in her relationship with Andrew, who would join her for lunch at Kingsbourne as soon as she returned from her holiday. 'It's just a piece of paper,' she said, trying to sound upbeat.

So, if nothing was to change, why the divorce? Their marriage had been through many trials, but I'm convinced that, in the back of both their minds, was the thought that one day they would be reconciled and live together again as husband and wife. Perhaps it was the thought of such a reconciliation that so worried those who drove Sarah and Andrew to the divorce court. They had seen an opportunity to rid themselves of the 'wretched Fergie' and they had seized it. Now she would be on her own again.

I later learned that the crucial talks, which led to the divorce announcement, took place over the Easter weekend at the couple's marital home, Sunninghill Park. Andrew and Sarah spent most of Saturday and Sunday discussing ways of making the best of what they both felt was an intolerable situation. They agreed, without any fuss from Andrew, that Sarah would have custody of the Princesses. To help ease her money troubles, she would live virtually on Andrew's doorstep, in a large stable block at Sunninghill that would be converted into a luxurious family home over the coming summer. The girls would never be very far from either their mother or father. It was an unusual arrangement for a divorcing couple, but one they both felt comfortable with. On Easter Monday Andrew drove to Windsor Castle to tell his parents what he and Sarah had decided and both said the arrangements met with their approval.

The divorce was listed as HRH The Duke of York *v* HRH The Duchess of York and scheduled for the following day at the Principal Registry of the High Court Family Division at Somerset House, London. It was the last on the list of 29 'quickie' special procedure divorces to be disposed of before Senior District Judge Gerald Angel.

Before flying out to Switzerland, Sarah had used a fountain pen and black ink to sign away her right to be called HRH together with the need for women to curtsy and men to bow before her. The signature was as bold and as strong as ever. Andrew had used the same pen formally to end the marriage in the drawing-room at Sunninghill Park.

Neither Sarah nor Andrew attended the hearing, the proceedings were over in less than three minutes and within six weeks they would no longer be husband and wife.

CHAPTER TWENTY-SIX
DOWNFALL OF A DUCHESS

The downfall of the Duchess of York was perhaps as inevitable as it was sad. What seemed like a marriage made in heaven was never really given a chance to work. Hindered considerably by Andrew's absence at sea and Sarah's inability to come to terms with the rigorous disciplines of Royal life, it probably never really stood a chance. By the time Andrew realised the errors of his ways and begged a neglected Sarah not to leave him, it was all, tragically, too late. He had shown his weakness by not standing up to those Sarah blamed for letting her down. As much as she loved him, Sarah doubted if he would ever be able to change.

Her arrival promised to breathe much-needed new life into the Royal Family — instead, it helped shake the Monarchy to its very foundations.

During nearly ten long and difficult years of marriage, a series of high-profile romances and exorbitant spending sprees brought Sarah the most hurtful and damaging public humiliation imaginable. Her seemingly thick skin, pierced more times than most could endure, belies the true Sarah Ferguson. Of course, much of the damage was self-inflicted. But I wonder how any independent young girl would be able to cope with life within what Sarah herself describes as 'the fantasy world' of the Royal Family in the 1990s. 'It's just not real,' she would often say. Looking for parallels, there is only Princess Diana and in her I see a desperately confused young woman driven to eating disorders and the brink of suicide by her husband's infidelity and the glare of the public spotlight.

The true Sarah is an attractive, caring and wonderful mother who, in her quest to be loved by everyone, somehow managed to lose her way in life and be used by men who were out for what they could get for themselves. Sarah did her best to fit into the Royal Family, but I often wonder whether she tried just a little bit too hard.

Sarah always vowed to be strong and not to bow to those who said 'no you can't, no you can't, no you can't'. In the end, not even she was strong enough.

I realise that people may criticise me for writing this book, but Sarah will never be given the opportunity fully to tell her side of the story or to reveal the full extent of the years of anguish and hurt she has endured.

Today, Sarah's dream is that a new white knight will magically appear and sweep her and her daughters away to a peaceful new life of love and happiness. I believe the dream will one day become reality and she will remarry, probably an older man and most likely an American. Of course, she and Andrew will remain good friends and the girls will grow up loving both of them, but Sarah *needs* a man in her life. She always has done, and she always will.

Sarah believes that Andrew will find happiness with another woman and settle down and remarry. She agrees with her father who said he believed the Duke had learned from his mistakes and would make a far better husband second time around. She really does want the best for him.

As for Sarah? Asked once what she would most like for company if she was stranded on a desert island, she replied, 'My children, of course; the Bible because you can read it and read it again ... and a man!' To me, that says it all.

SINS AND SCANDALS!
GO BEHIND THE SCENES WITH PINNACLE

JULIA: THE UNTOLD STORY OF AMERICA'S
PRETTY WOMAN   (898, $4.99)
by Aileen Joyce

She lit up the screen in STEEL MAGNOLIAS and PRETTY WOMAN. She's been paired with scores of stunning leading men. And now, here's an explosive unauthorized biography of Julia Roberts that tells all. Read about Julia's recent surprise marriage to Lyle Lovitt—Her controversial two-year disappearance—Her big comeback that has Tinseltown talking—and much, much more!

SEAN CONNERY: FROM 007 TO
HOLLYWOOD ICON   (742, $4.50)
by Andrew Rule

After nearly thirty years—and countless films—Sean Connery is still one of the most irresistible and bankable stars in Hollywood. Now, for the first time, go behind the scenes to meet the man behind the suave 007 myth. From his beginnings in a Scotland slum to international stardom, take an intimate look at this most fascinating and exciting superstar.

HOWARD STERN: BIG MOUTH   (796, $4.99)
by Jeff Menell

Brilliant, stupid, sexist, racist, obscene, hilarious—and just plain gross! Howard Stern is the man you love to hate. Now you can find out the real story behind morning radio's number one bad boy!

THE "I HATE BRENDA" BOOK   (797, $4.50)
By Michael Carr & Darby

From the editors of the official "I HATE BRENDA" newsletter comes everything you ever wanted to know about Shannen Doherty. Here's the dirt on a young woman who seems to be careening through the heady galaxy of Hollywood, a burning asteroid spinning "out of control!"

THE RICHEST GIRL IN THE WORLD   (792, $4.99)
by Stephanie Mansfield

At the age of thirteen, Doris Duke inherited a $100 million tobacco fortune. By the time she was thirty, Doris Duke had lavished millions on her lovers and husbands. An eccentric who thumbed her nose at society, Duke's circle of friends included Jackie Onassis, Macolm Forbes, Truman Capote, Andy Warhol and Imelda Marcos. But all the money in the world couldn't buy the love that she searched for!

Available wherever paperbacks are sold, or order direct from the Publisher. Send cover price plus 50¢ per copy for mailing and handling to Penguin USA, P.O. Box 999, c/o Dept. 17109, Bergenfield, NJ 07621. Residents of New York and Tennessee must include sales tax. DO NOT SEND CASH.

INFORMATIVE—
COMPELLING—
SCINTILLATING—
NON-FICTION FROM PINNACLE TELLS THE TRUTH!

BORN TOO SOON (751, $4.50)
by Elizabeth Mehren

This is the poignant story of Elizabeth's daughter Emily's premature birth. As the parents of one of the 275,000 babies born prematurely each year in this country, she and her husband were plunged into the world of the Neonatal Intensive Care unit. With stunning candor, Elizabeth Mehren relates her gripping story of unshakable faith and hope—and of courage that comes in tiny little packages.

THE PROSTATE PROBLEM (745, $4.50)
by Chet Cunningham

An essential, easy-to-use guide to the treatment and prevention of the illness that's in the headlines. This book explains in clear, practical terms all the facts. Complete with a glossary of medical terms, and a comprehensive list of health organizations and support groups, this illustrated handbook will help men combat prostate disorder and lead longer, healthier lives.

THE ACADEMY AWARDS HANDBOOK (0258, $4.99)

An interesting and easy-to-use guide for movie fans everywhere, the book features a year-to-year listing of all the Oscar nominations in every category, all the winners, an expert analysis of who wins and why, a complete index to get information quickly, and even a 99% foolproof method to pick this year's winners!

WHAT WAS HOT (894, $4.50)
by Julian Biddle

Journey through 40 years of the trends and fads, famous and infamous figures, and momentous milestones in American history. From hoola hoops to rap music, greasers to yuppies, Elvis to Madonna—it's all here, trivia for all ages. An entertaining and evocative overview of the milestones in America from the 1950's to the 1990's!

Available wherever paperbacks are sold, or order direct from the Publisher. Send cover price plus 50¢ per copy for mailing and handling to Penguin USA, P.O. Box 999, c/o Dept. 17109, Bergenfield, NJ 07621. Residents of New York and Tennessee must include sales tax. DO NOT SEND CASH.

DANGEROUS GAMES   (0-7860-0270-0, $4.99)
by Amanda Scott

When Nicholas Barrington, eldest son of the Earl of Ulcombe, first met Melissa Seacort, the desperation he sensed beneath her well-bred beauty haunted him. He didn't realize how desperate Melissa really was . . . until he found her again at a Newmarket gambling club—being auctioned off by her father to the highest bidder. So, Nick bought himself a wife. With a villain hot on their heels, and a fortune and their lives at stake, they would gamble everything on the most dangerous game of all: love.

A TOUCH OF PARADISE   (0-7860-0271-9, $4.99)
by Alexa Smart

As a confidence man and scam runner in 1880s America, Malcolm Northrup has amassed a fortune. Now, posing as the eminent Sir John Abbot—scholar, and possible discoverer of the lost continent of Atlantis—he's taking his act on the road with a lecture tour, seeking funds for a scientific experiment he has no intention of making. But scholar Halia Davenport is determined to accompany Malcolm on his "expedition" . . . even if she must kidnap him!

Available wherever paperbacks are sold, or order direct from the Publisher. Send cover price plus 50¢ per copy for mailing and handling to Penguin USA, P.O. Box 999, c/o Dept. 17109, Bergenfield, NJ 07621. Residents of New York and Tennessee must include sales tax. DO NOT SEND CASH.